CAMBRIDGE CLASSICAL STUDIES

General Editors
J. A. CROOK, E. J. KENNEY, A. M. SNODGRASS

A STUDY OF *DAPHNIS & CHLOE*

A STUDY OF *DAPHNIS & CHLOE*

R. L. HUNTER
Fellow of Pembroke College, Cambridge

CAMBRIDGE UNIVERSITY PRESS
CAMBRIDGE
LONDON   NEW YORK   NEW ROCHELLE
MELBOURNE   SYDNEY

CAMBRIDGE UNIVERSITY PRESS
Cambridge, New York, Melbourne, Madrid, Cape Town, Singapore, São Paulo

Cambridge University Press
The Edinburgh Building, Cambridge CB2 8RU, UK

Published in the United States of America by Cambridge University Press, New York

www.cambridge.org
Information on this title: www.cambridge.org/9780521254526

First published 1983
This digitally printed version 2007

A catalogue record for this publication is available from the British Library

Library of Congress Catalogue Card Number: 83–3928

ISBN 978-0-521-25452-6 hardback
ISBN 978-0-521-04137-9 paperback

CONTENTS

PREFACE

The prose fiction of antiquity has been the subject of increasing scholarly attention in the last twenty-five years, and *Daphnis & Chloe* has benefited from this general revival of interest. Nevertheless, critical progress has been hindered by the lack of a basic guide to the literary and rhetorical background against which this work was written. The present essay is an attempt to fill that gap. I have tried to combine information of a kind which is usually found in a continuous commentary with an outline of the various interpretative directions in which that information points. About the 'origins of the Greek Novel', the problem which has dominated scholarship in this field ever since the publication of Erwin Rohde's magnificent study *Der griechische Roman und seine Vorläufer*, I have said very little, although Longus' exploitation of the traditions of historiography and comedy serves as a reminder of two major influences on the fiction of later antiquity. My silence on this subject will, I hope, suggest that it is unhelpful to view *Daphnis & Chloe* as 'the standard ancient novel' relocated in a pastoral setting and that a solution to the problem of the origins of the genre as a whole is unlikely also to supply the key to an appreciation of a particular example of the genre. The Greek novels which survive in a manuscript tradition differ from each other so widely in terms of wit, rhetorical skill and narrative coherence that, even after the standard division into pre-sophistic (Xenophon of Ephesus, Chariton) and sophistic (Achilles Tatius, Longus, Heliodorus), it makes very little sense to treat them as though they were almost identical specimens off a production-line.

I am rather less happy that I have had little to say about the relationship between the world presented in *Daphnis & Chloe* and rural life on the Aegean islands in the second and

third centuries A.D. Even if, however, I were fully competent
to discuss the social and economic history of the Roman
Empire, it may be doubted whether prolonged consideration
of this topic would prove very fruitful. Longus presents us
with a stylised picture of rural life on an island famous for
poetry and wine, and this picture is consistent and, in its
own literary and rhetorical context, plausible. Analysis of
Daphnis & Chloe can, of course, tell us something about
attitudes towards the countryside in the period in which it
was written, although it is in other respects so individual a
work that we should be cautious about using it as a representative expression of the views of a whole social class.

In preparing this study I have incurred a number of debts
which I here gratefully acknowledge. Michael Reeve kindly
sent me a copy of his text of Longus before its publication,
and Ewen Bowie's comments on the penultimate version of
this essay identified many obscurities and saved me from
several errors. Susan Moore guided the book through the
final stages of preparation with her habitual care and acumen.
I wish to thank the General Editors of Cambridge Classical
Studies and the Faculty Board of Classics for undertaking
the publication of this work and, in particular, Professor
E. J. Kenney for his assistance and encouragement. Four
institutions have put me deeply in their debt: the British
Academy, which provided financial assistance towards a
period of research abroad; the Fondation Hardt in Geneva,
where that research was conducted in ideal surroundings;
the Cambridge University Press, which has handled this book
and its author with enviable skill; and Pembroke College, for
whose continued kindnesses this slim volume is scant reward.
If she had allowed it, my largest debt of all would have
been acknowledged in the dedication of this book to my wife.

Cambridge   R.L.H.
April, 1983

REFERENCES AND ABBREVIATIONS

I abbreviate *Daphnis and Chloe* to *D&C* and cite it in Reeve's text; the editions of *D&C* of Villoison (Paris 1778), Seiler (Leipzig 1835), Edmonds (Cambridge, Mass.–London 1916), Dalmeyda (Paris 1934), Schönberger (Berlin 1960) and Reeve (Leipzig 1983) are cited by editor's name only. Lyric poets are cited in the continuous numeration of D. L. Page, *Poetae melici Graeci* (Oxford 1962) and epigrammatists both by the conventional reference and (where applicable) by the continuous numeration of A. S. F. Gow and D. L. Page, *Hellenistic epigrams* (Cambridge 1965) and *The Garland of Philip and some contemporary epigrams* (Cambridge 1968), *HE* and *GP* respectively. In the case of fragmentary texts I give the editor's name after the reference.

Standard abbreviations are used for periodicals and works of reference; modern books and articles which are cited more than once are listed in the bibliography at the end of the work and are cited in the notes by author's name and date, e.g. Chalk [1960].

CHAPTER ONE

TITLE, AUTHOR, DATE

The manuscripts of Longus' novel most commonly refer to the work as ποιμενικὰ τὰ περὶ [or κατὰ] Δάφνιν καὶ Χλόην or simply ποιμενικά, but once as αἰπολικὰ τὰ κατὰ Χλόην καὶ Δάφνιν and (in the colophon in the Florentine manuscript) as ποιμενικὰ τὰ περὶ Δάφνιν καὶ Χλόην Λεσβιακὰ ἐρωτικά. In the manuscript tradition, the novels of Xenophon of Ephesus (τὰ κατὰ Ἀνθίαν καὶ Ἀβροκόμην Ἐφεσιακά) and Heliodorus (ἡ Χαρίκλεια, τὰ περὶ Θεαγένην καὶ Χαρίκλειαν or Αἰθιοπικὰ τὰ περὶ Θεαγένην καὶ Χαρίκλειαν) share with *D&C* a system of naming both by description and from the principal characters, whereas the novels of Chariton and Achilles Tatius are designated only by the names of the characters. The fact that later Byzantine novelists seem to have used only the personal naming system and that a scrap from a late second-century A.D. text of the novel of Lollianus (fr. A2a *verso* Henrichs) calls that work Φοινικικά might suggest that most novels were originally given (presumably by their authors) descriptive titles such as Ἐφεσιακά or Αἰθιοπικά and that the personal titles came into use later.[1] If this is correct, then the original title of *D&C* was Λεσβιακά or ποιμενικά or Λεσβιακὰ ποιμενικά, and it is relevant here to note that the final words of the novel are ποιμένων παίγνια. With ποιμενικά may be compared the title of Petronius' comic romance, if that has been correctly explained as σατυρικά (i.e. σατυρικῶν *libri*):[2] both of these titles keep the form of a 'local' title such as Ἐφεσιακά (a form ultimately derived from epic and historiography) but are purely descriptive. Nevertheless, it seems improbable that one style only was in use in antiquity and that the others are wholly Byzantine or mediaeval. The evidence of the fragment of the Φοινικικά is perhaps weakened by the obviously comic (as opposed to idealising) nature of that novel, and a second-century A.D. text of Chariton refers

1

to that novel as τὰ περὶ Κα[λλιρόην] διηγήματα (P. Michael-
idae 1).[3] The analogy of dramatic scripts for tragedies,
comedies and mimes and of philosophical works, which
often have two or more designations by which they were
known either popularly or in the scholarly tradition, suggests
that Longus' ancient readers probably used more than one
title when discussing or citing the work. The analogy of
comedies and tragedies is particularly suggestive, as these
were often popularly called after their leading characters
even when they were entered in competition under a less
informative title (such as a description of the chorus).[4] It is,
of course, not hard to see why readers would refer to Longus'
novel as τὰ περὶ Δάφνιν καὶ Χλόην, whatever title the author
had given it. Chariton himself ends his work with the words
τοσάδε περὶ Καλλιρόης συνέγραψα.

The manuscripts of D&C give the author's name as Λόγγος.[5]
The fact that this is a Roman name does not necessarily mean
that the author was a native Italian, who wrote in Greek, as
Greek families and individuals regularly adopted the names
of their Roman patrons, but the possibility that Longus was
an Italian writing in Greek must be considered, although it
seems a slight one in view of his polished style.[6] Moreover,
an extant list of important citizens of Mytilene from the time
of the late Republic or early Empire includes a Γν. Πομπήιος
Λόγγος (IG XII.2.88) and another inscription of uncertain
date records an ἀρχιερεύς of Mytilene called Αὖλος Πο[μπήϊ]ος
Διονυσ[όδωρ]ος (IG XII.2.249). In view of the lack of other
evidence, there would seem no reason not to seize this
information and conclude, as did Cichorius,[7] that the author
of D&C was a member of this important Graeco-Roman
family, which was a distinguished one indeed if the [C.?]
Pompeius Longus Gallus who was consul in A.D. 49 (PIR
III p. 67) was a member of it. If this conclusion is correct,
then the ignorance of a local legend which the narrator claims
in the preface, and the very phrase ἐν Λέσβωι, would not
imply, as they might otherwise seem to do, that the author
was not a native of Lesbos, but simply that he is writing for a
wide readership. There is nothing in the novel that suggests

that Longus was unacquainted with the island on which he set his story, and indeed some scholars have argued that the book reveals accurate and detailed knowledge of the topography of the interior of Lesbos (cf. below pp. 21–2).[8] However that may be, it does seem very likely that the author had a personal connection with Lesbos.

D&C has from time to time been dated to every Christian century from the second to the sixth. As there is no external evidence for this work before the twelfth century[9] and, on any reckoning, very little internal evidence, it is not surprising that opinions have ranged widely. Most critics would now probably place Longus in the centre of the 'Second Sophistic', a movement which is usually regarded as a phenomenon of the period A.D. *c.* 50–250.[10] Of the other novelists it is Achilles Tatius who most obviously shares the 'sophistic' features of Longus' style, and Achilles' novel must be dated no later than the second half of the second century, as a papyrus text has demonstrated.[11] Although both writers tell the tale of Pan and Syrinx (2.34 ~ Ach. Tat. 8.6.7–10) there is nothing in the two passages which strongly suggests that one is borrowing from the other,[12] and the fact that both works contain such sophistic set pieces as the description of a luxurious garden means nothing in the context of this rhetorical prose.[13] Three arguments of varying cogency have recently been advanced to support the scholarly intuition that *D&C* is to be dated to the late second or early third century A.D., and these arguments must now be reviewed. I preface my survey with the observation that there is no sign that Longus sought to produce rhythmical *clausulae* based on accentual patterns, although most Greek prose from about A.D. 350 onwards shows clear signs of this development.[14] This is perhaps as good a reason as any to dismiss the very late dates in the 400s and 500s which have sometimes been proposed.

In 3.27–30 the Nymphs make Daphnis a present of a purse containing 3000 drachmas from the wreck of the ship which had belonged to the young men of Methymna; with this money he is to bid for Chloe's hand. In the context of the novel this is a sum which is fantastically large for Dryas and Nape (cf. 3.30.1), but one which the young men had left lying around on the ship and which Dionysophanes gives (with no obvious difficulty but some generosity) to Dryas to match Daphnis' gift (4.33.2). Scholars have noted that these facts would not suit a time in the last third of the third century or later when the rampant inflation of the Empire would have made 3000 dr. virtually worthless.[15] This argument deserves to be taken seriously as there is no reason why Dionysophanes' generosity should be impugned and the stupidity of the other characters highlighted in this way. The period A.D. *c.* 100–260 would, however, be a suitable one: in the second century the cost of an adult male slave, on our present evidence, varied from 500 to 2800 drachmas, and in the first half of the third century the average was somewhat nearer 2000.[16] A sum amounting to the purchase price of two slaves seems to suit the novel's requirements. The major doubt about this argument arises from the fact that a great deal of the sophistic literature of the Empire takes as its setting the golden age of Athens in the fifth and fourth centuries B.C.,[17] and although Longus' novel is not tightly tied to any particular time and is certainly not consistently anachronistic, there are a few features which do suggest that Longus was not untouched by this habit of setting oneself in the past.[18] We may, therefore, wish to explain the figure of 3000 drachmas as a nostalgic anachronism composed in an age of great inflation, if indeed it is not to be considered simply as a conveniently round sum.[19]

A second clue upon which great weight has recently been placed was first suggested by Otto Weinreich.[20] He noted an affinity between *D&C* and Roman landscape painting of the middle of the second century A.D., a style of painting whose popularity does not seem to have continued into the third century;[21] Perry[22] added the observation that more bucolic literature, as well as art, survives from the second and early third centuries than from the later period and we know that interest in the work of Theocritus was keen in the first two centuries of the Empire.[23] The suggested connection with art is very welcome in view of the fact that *D&C* is presented as an account of a marvellous painting, and there certainly is a sense in which the episodic structure of the novel (cf. below pp. 65–6) may be compared to 'narrative' painting in which the same figures recur in a series of disparate but related scenes.[24] Even if, however, this affinity is sufficient to forbid a date after, say, A.D. 250, I doubt that it can be used to fix a date with any precision within the two and a half preceding centuries. The landscapes from the middle of the second century are not obviously more like scenes from Longus than are the landscapes from first-century Pompeii, and there is no reason to doubt that at any time within this period a writer of bucolic literature would have been able to find suitable paintings from which to draw inspiration, should he wish to do so. A more general objection to attempts at a narrow dating on these grounds may be drawn from the nature of rural description itself. City-dwellers of later antiquity, like their counterparts today, were apt to think of the country-side in terms of idyllic and static scenes – cattle lowing, rivers babbling, happy harvesters and so on. In ancient literature we may trace this from the rural scenes on the Shield of Achilles (*Iliad* 18.541–86) to the rhetorical ἐκφράσεις of the late Empire. A similarity between landscape painting and highly sophisticated literary descriptions of the countryside ought not to surprise us when viewed in this context. It is interesting that a recent attempt has been made to link the poetry of Tibullus with contemporary landscape painting.[25] Like Longus, Tibullus combined originally pastoral themes with erotic ones,[26] and the two writers also share certain details and vignettes: the simple piety of the Tibullan *persona* who honours all religious totems in the fields and always offers first fruits to the gods (1.1.11ff.) is matched by the piety of Daphnis and Chloe towards the Nymphs (cf. 2.2.4–6 where the children bring ἀπαρχὰς τοῦ τρυγητοῦ) and recalls the religious motifs common in Roman landscape paintings. The idea of lovers living a simple, rural life together occurs at Tib. 1.2.71–4 and in 1.5 Tibullus imagines Delia and himself as a happy, rustic couple (vv. 23–4 in which

Delia helps Tibullus with the vintage recall Longus 2.1.3). I am not, of course, suggesting that Longus is indebted to Tibullus nor am I concerned here with the likely use of common sources, but I wish merely to note the similar tone and style of this aspect of the two writers and to suggest on the basis of this similarity that an affinity between *D&C* and some forms of landscape painting is not a very solid criterion for dating the novel. Both bucolic painting and post-Theocritean bucolic literature greatly simplify life in the countryside and it is not surprising that each presents a similar vision.[27]

A relative date for *D&C* has been sought by considering the possible significance of certain parallels between it and the *Letters* of Alciphron.[28] Unfortunately, Alciphron's date is itself a thorny problem, and the whole method of relative dating by arguments for literary dependence is open to suspicion when so much literature has been lost and we are dealing with works which constantly repeat the same motifs and ideas.[29] As, however, standard modern works still refer to and use the results of investigations of this kind I hope that a new and complete survey will not be out of place here. My discussion will be divided into a consideration of names common to the two writers, then words and phrases in common and finally motifs and scenes in common.

Reich[30] calculated that of twenty-six proper names in *D&C* four also occur in Alciphron (Hippasos, Alc. 3.12; Gnathon, Alc. 2.32; Megacles, Alc. 3.25 and Philopoimen, Alc. 2.21), and three other Longan names appear in Alciphron in extended forms (Nape as Napaios and Eunape, Alc. 2.17 and 2.18, Dryas as Dryades and Dryantidas, Alc. 2.39 and 2.8, and Agele as Agelarchidas, Alc. 2.5). Of the letters in which these characters appear only two have any other connection with Longus: with Alc. 2.18 may be compared Longus 4.8.4 (cf. below pp. 12–13), and Alc. 2.8 has a not very striking verbal coincidence with Longus 2.39.3.[31] Of the shared names Gnathon[32] and Megacles[33] are so common as to prove nothing, Philopoimen was a famous historical name which might have occurred to any bucolic writer and there seems no reason why the possibly fictitious actor called Hippasos of Ambracia whom Alciphron mentions at 3.12.1 should have anything to do with Longus' Mytilenean general. Hippasos is in any event not a rare name. Reich placed great weight on the fact that Alciphron always has the longer (and hence, in Reich's view, secondary) formation. Even if this were strictly true,[34] it is hard to see that much can be made of it: I consider elsewhere the personal names in *D&C* (cf. below pp. 16–17), but here it may be observed that with his penchant for *redende Namen* Alciphron was quite capable of inventing all of the relevant names himself, and none of them is so striking as to suggest dependence upon Longus. Rather than considering the names simply in terms of length, we ought to think of Alciphron as concerned to produce recognisable personal endings and formations (patronymics etc.), whereas Longus was simply interested in the fairy-tale aspects of these names.[35]

Of the words and phrases which Longus and Alciphron share, only the following call for special comment: (i) Longus 2.5.1 and Alc. 3.12.4 both describe mocking laughter as καπυρός, and this epithet is used of laughter elsewhere only at Nossis, *AP* 7.414.1 (= *HE* 2827) which is an epitaph for the comic poet Rhinthon. The meaning of καπυρός has been very much discussed[36] but, whatever its precise connotation in this context, it is perhaps dangerous to believe that it was as rare as our texts seem to suggest. (ii) The adjective μεσαιπόλιος occurs at Longus 4.13.2 and Alc. 2.22.2 and 3.13.2. Both writers may be echoing Hom. *Il.* 13.361 and doing so independently, but this word does seem to have enjoyed a certain currency in later Greek: to LSJ *s.v.* add Philostr. *Vit.Soph.* pp. 568 and 599 and Aelian, *NA* 12.43.[37] (iii) Both Longus (4.20.1) and Alciphron (2.16.2) use the phrase τοξοποιεῖν τὰς ὀφρῦς (τὴν ὀφρῦν in Longus), which occurs elsewhere in extant literature only at Ar. *Lys.* 8. That both borrow from Aristophanes and do so independently is certainly not incredible,[38] and it is regularly overlooked that at 4.7.8, οὐ πρέπει σκυθρωποῖς εἶναι τοιούτοις ὄμμασι, Alciphron is probably again echoing this same passage of

Aristophanes, μὴ σκυθρώπαζ' ὦ τέκνον. |οὐ γὰρ πρέπει σοι τοξοποιεῖν τὰς ὀφρῦς. That the manuscripts of Alciphron reproduce the Aristophanic and expected plural τὰς ὀφρῦς (cf. LSJ s.v.) whereas Longus has τὴν ὀφρῦν may be significant, but could in fact be used to argue for the priority of either author. In short, this coincidence between the two writers is of little assistance in determining a relative date for them.

In considering the passages where similarity of scene or motif has been thought significant I follow the order of Reich's discussion.[39]

In 4.15 Daphnis demonstrates the musical abilities of his flock for the benefit of Cleariste:

ὁ δὲ καθίσας αὐτοὺς ὥσπερ θέατρον στὰς ὑπὸ τῆι φηγῶι καὶ ἐκ τῆς πήρας τὴν σύριγγα προκομίσας πρῶτα μὲν ὀλίγον ἐνέπνευσε, καὶ αἱ αἶγες ἔστησαν τὰς κεφαλὰς ἀράμεναι · εἶτα ἐνέπνευσε τὸ νόμιον, καὶ αἱ αἶγες ἐνέμοντο νεύσασαι κάτω · αὖθις λιγυρὸν ἐνέδωκε, καὶ ἀθρόαι κατεκλίθησαν · ἐσύρισέ τι καὶ ὀξὺ μέλος, αἱ δὲ ὥσπερ λύκου προσιόντος εἰς τὴν ὕλην κατέφυγον · μετ᾽ ὀλίγον ἀνακλητικὸν ἐφθέγξατο, καὶ ἐξελθοῦσαι τῆς ὕλης πλησίον αὐτοῦ τῶν ποδῶν συνέδραμον. οὐδὲ ἀνθρώπους οἰκέτας εἶδεν ἄν τις οὕτω πειθομένους προστάγματι δεσπότου. οἵ τε οὖν ἄλλοι πάντες ἐθαύμαζον καὶ πρὸ πάντων ἡ Κλεαρίστη, καὶ τὰ δῶρα ἀποδώσειν ὤμοσε καλῶι τε ὄντι αἰπόλωι καὶ μουσικῶι ·

With this scene may be compared Alc. 2.9:

Πρατίνας Ἐπιγόνωι

μεσημβρίας οὔσης σταθερᾶς φιλήνεμόν τινα ἐπιλεξάμενος πίτυν καὶ πρὸς τὰς αὔρας ἐκκεκλιμένην, ὑπὸ ταύτηι τὸ καῦμα ἐσκέπαζον. καί μοι ψυχάζοντι μάλ᾽ ἡδέως ἐπῆλθέ τι καὶ μουσικῆς ἐπαφήσασθαι, καὶ λαβὼν τὴν σύριγγα ἐπέτρεχον τῆι γλώττηι, στενὸν τὸ πνεῦμα μετὰ τῶν χειλέων ἐπισύρων, καί μοι ἡδύ τι καὶ νόμιον ἐξηκούετο μέλος. ἐν τούτωι δὲ οὐκ οἶδ᾽ ὅπως ὑπὸ τῆς ἡδυφωνίας θελγόμεναι πᾶσαί μοι πανταχόθεν αἱ αἶγες περιεχύθησαν, καὶ ἀφεῖσαι νέμεσθαι τοὺς κομάρους καὶ τὸν ἀνθέρικον ὅλαι τοῦ μέλους ἐγίνοντο. ἐγὼ δὲ ἐν μέσαις τὸν Ἡδωνὸν ἐμμούμην τὸν παῖδα τῆς Καλλιόπης. ταῦτά σε οὖν εὐαγγελίζομαι, φίλον ἄνδρα συνειδέναι βουλόμενος ὅτι μοι μουσικόν ἐστιν τὸ αἰπόλιον.

The most striking verbal similarity does not in fact occur in the directly comparable scenes but rather immediately before

8

the Longan passage when Lamon tells his master that Daphnis has made his goats μουσικάς (cf. Alc. μουσικόν ἐστιν τὸ αἰπόλιον); there are general similarities also with the descriptions of σῦριγξ-playing at Longus 1.24.4 and 2.35.2–3[40] and with the activities of the girl who was metamorphosed into the φάττα (1.27.2). In another context I have referred to the 'Orphic' background to this scene in Longus and to the literary tradition which lies behind it (below pp. 30–1);[41] this tradition must inevitably weaken arguments for dependence of one author upon another here, but I would also make three specific points.

In view of what will be said below about the status of the πίτυς in these authors, it is worth pointing out that this tree is perfectly appropriate in Alc. 2.9. This epistle is far more 'idyllic' than most of the *Letters of farmers* and the πίτυς is a standard feature of the idyllic countryside; in particular the πίτυς is an obvious tree under which to seek shade and rest at midday, cf. Prop. 2.34.67, 3.13.37, Hor. *C.* 2.3.9, Libanius 8.266.1 F, Myrinus, *AP* 7.703 (= *GP* 2568) Θύρσις ὁ κωμήτης ... ὁ συρίζων Πανὸς ἴσον δόνακι | ἔνδιος οἰνοπότης σκιερὰν ὑπὸ τὰν πίτυν εὕδει κτλ. Moreover, this tree may also be in place here in a context of rustic piping because of the special relationship between Pan, Pitys and the winds (for which cf. below p. 53). The appearance of the πίτυς in Alciphron 2.9 cannot therefore be used to argue that that letter is indebted to *D&C*. Secondly, Dalmeyda noted that, whereas in Longus τὸ νόμιον must mean 'the tune which gives the signal for τὸ νέμειν', in Alciphron ἡδύ τι καὶ νόμιον ἐξηκούετο μέλος means simply 'I heard a sweet pastoral tune', and he argued from this that Alciphron has borrowed a detail from Longus but has lost the original force of that detail. νόμιον μέλος does, however, occur at Ap. Rhod. 1.578 in a passage where the playing of Orpheus is compared to that of a shepherd leading his sheep, and in that passage the phrase must mean 'a pastoral tune' in a quite general sense, particularly as the shepherd is leading his flock back to the fold after τὸ νέμειν has been completed. Finally, Dalmeyda stressed that 2.9 differs from most of the *Letters of farmers* in that the chief character and writer of the epistle does not seem very much at home in the countryside.

It is, however, important to remember that this epistle belongs with the tradition of idyllic, bucolic writings whereas most of these letters remind one rather of the attitude to the countryside and those who live there which is adopted in the New Comedy. The names of the author and recipient of this letter, Pratinas and Epigonus, were clearly chosen to recall two famous musicians of archaic Greece,[42] Pratinas perhaps being selected because of his well known association with the rather rustic genre of satyr-drama. In short, although the rather exceptional character of 2.9 could be explained on the hypothesis that Alciphron has drawn his inspiration from Longus (or indeed from a third lost source), it is just as likely that the unusual features are the result of the fact that Alciphron is here experimenting in a different tradition, that of the bucolic idyll.

The next[43] set of passages to be considered are the descriptions of Daphnis' hunting expedition in the third book (3.5–11) and Alc. 2.27:

Ἀμπελίων Εὐέργωι

πολὺς ὁ χειμὼν τὸ τῆτες καὶ οὐδενί* ἐξιτητόν. πάντα γὰρ ἡ χιὼν κατείληφε, καὶ λευκανθίζουσιν οὐχ οἱ λόφοι μόνον ἀλλὰ καὶ τὰ κοῖλα τῆς γῆς, ἀπορία δὲ ἔργων, ἀργὸν δὲ καθίζειν ὄνειδος. προκύψας δῆτα τῆς καλύβης οὐκ ἔφθην παρανοίξας τὸ θύριον καὶ ὁρῶ σὺν τῶι νιφετῶι δῆμον ὅλον ὀρνέων φερόμενον, καὶ κοψίχους καὶ κίχλας. εὐθέως οὖν ἀπὸ τῆς λεκάνης ἀνασπάσας ἰξὸν ἐπαλείφω τῶν ἀχράδων τοὺς κλάδους, καὶ ὅσον οὔπω τὸ νέφος ἐπέστη τῶν στρουθίων καὶ πᾶσαι ἐκ τῶν ὁροδάμνων ἐκρέμαντο, θέαμα ἡδύ, πτερῶν ἐχόμεναι καὶ κεφαλῆς καὶ ποδῶν εἰλημμέναι. ἐκ τούτων λάχος σοι τὰς πίονας καὶ εὐσάρκους ἀπέσταλκα πέντε καὶ εἴκοσι. κοινωνεῖν γὰρ ἀγαθὸν τοῖς ἀγαθοῖς, φθονοῦσι δὲ οἱ πονηροὶ τῶν γειτόνων.

* οὐδὲ ⟨κυ⟩νὶ M. L. West, cf. Men. *Misoumenos* A15–16 Turner.

The only verbal parallel worth noting is that in both passages the characters catch κίχλαι and κόψιχοι, although in Longus these are only part of a longer list (3.5.2). This similarity is, however, not really significant as these two species are often named together in extant literature and are, as Longus 3.5.2

10

puts it, χειμεριυοὶ ὄρυιθες.[44] The descriptions of winter in Alciphron and in Longus 3.3 are quite unlike in all but general tone,[45] and the common tradition which lies behind both authors may be illustrated by Horace's account of the countryside in winter:

> at cum tonantis annus hibernus Iouis
>   imbris niuesque comparat,
> aut trudit acris hinc et hinc multa cane
>   apros in obstantis plagas,
> aut amite leui rara tendit retia,
>   turdis edacibus dolos,
> pauidumque leporem et aduenam laqueo gruem
>   iucunda captat praemia.   (*Epode* 2.29–36)

Horace's countryman catches *turdi* (i.e. κίχλαι), as do Longus' and Alciphron's, and in ancient technical treatises on fowling winter is recommended as the appropriate time for this activity.[46] There are two further motifs which these passages of Alciphron and Longus share. One is the very common idea that winter is the idle time for farmers;[47] it is to be noted, however, that Alciphron uses the Hesiodic version of this idea, i.e. farmers ought not to be idle in winter (*WD* 493–501), and ἀργὸν δὲ καθίζειν ὄνειδος in Alciphron's letter looks like an echo of *WD* 311 ἔργον δ' οὐδὲν ὄνειδος, ἀεργίη δέ τ' ὄνειδος. We cannot, therefore, attach any significance to the fact that Longus and Alciphron share this motif. The other shared motif is that of generosity to friends (cf. Longus 3.11.2), but this is again not very significant as Alciphron uses this idea frequently (cf. 2.20, 2.29, 3.10) and it is a common one in accounts of the simple and virtuous life of the countryside: the generosity with which Dio is treated by the Euboean hunters in Oration 7 (on which cf. below pp. 66–7) may serve as a representative example. In short, a convincing case for interdependence between Longus and Alciphron in these passages cannot be made.[48]

Reich next pointed to Longus 3.16.1 where Lycaenion escapes from her house allegedly on the same errand as the lady who writes Alc. 2.7, ὠδίνουσά με ἀρτίως ἥκειν ὡς ἑαυτὴν ἡ τοῦ γείτονος μετέπεμψε γυνή. Behind these passages

11

seems to lie Ar. *Eccl.* 528–9 where Praxagora covers her trip to the assembly by telling Blepyrus, γυνή μέ τις νύκτωρ ἑταίρα καὶ φίλη | μετεπέμψατ' ὠδίνουσα. Blepyrus suspects that Praxagora has really been visiting a lover and in Longus this is indeed what Lycaenion leaves her home to do. Alciphron has, on the other hand, reversed the motif: the trip to assist at a birth is no longer a pretext to get out of the house but a genuine errand by a midwife who is then stopped on her way by an old man with sexual designs upon her. Whether Alciphron's more imaginative use of the Aristophanic motif suggests anything about the relationship between Longus and Alciphron must be at least doubtful, but if one has adapted the other's work here, it seems more likely that Alciphron's 'improved' version is the later of the two.

The final pair of passages to be considered is 4.8.4 where Lamon expresses his anxiety at what his master will do when he sees the garden which Lampis has destroyed, κρεμᾶι γέροντα ἄνθρωπον ἐκ μιᾶς πίτυος ὡς Μαρσύαν, τάχα δὲ καὶ Δάφνιν ὡς τῶν αἰγῶν ταῦτα εἰργασμένων, and Alc. 2.18:

Εὐνάπη Γλαύκηι

ὁ μὲν ἀνὴρ ἀπόδημός ἐστί μοι τρίτην ταύτην ἡμέραν ἔχων ἐν ἄστει, ὁ δὲ θητεύων παρ' ἡμῖν Παρμένων ζημία καθαρά, ῥάιθυμος ἄνθρωπος καὶ τὰ πολλὰ καταπίπτων εἰς ὕπνον. ὁ δὲ λύκος ἀργαλέος πάροικος βλέπων φονῶδές τι καὶ αἱμοβόρον · Χιόνην γὰρ τὴν καλλιστεύουσαν τῶν αἰγῶν ἐκ τοῦ φελλέως ἁρπάσας οἴχεται · καὶ ὁ μὲν δειπνεῖ ἀγαθὴν αἶγα καὶ εὐγάλακτον, ἐγὼ δὲ δάκρυα τῶν ὀφθαλμῶν ἀπολείβω. πέπυσται δὲ τούτων οὐδὲν ὁ ἀνήρ · εἰ δὲ μάθοι, κρεμήσεται μὲν ἐκ τῆς πλησίον πίτυος ὁ μισθωτός, αὐτὸς δὲ οὐ πρότερον ἀνήσει πάντα μηχανώμενος, πρὶν τὰς παρὰ τοῦ λύκου δίκας εἰσπράξασθαι.

In addition to the general similarity of the two passages, two specific points have been made by earlier critics. Reich observed that although Longus frequently refers to the pine-tree, the only other reference in Alciphron is 2.9.1, a passage which I have considered above, and he concluded that Alciphron has here borrowed from Longus. Bonner[49] noted that the name Πιτυΐσκος occurs at *Epist.* 2.20, but most critics have accepted the validity of Reich's observation:[50]

as legend made it a pine-tree from which Marsyas was hung,[51] Alciphron seems to have borrowed a detail and yet again lost the original force of that detail. There are, however, serious objections to this argument. Alciphron in fact mentions very few trees in the *Letters of farmers* and none more often than twice.[52] There is moreover a certain attraction in Bonner's suggestion that, because of the various legends associated with it, the pine was an 'unlucky' tree and that ἐκ πίτυος κρεμᾶσθαι may be semi-proverbial. Secondly, Dalmeyda observed that Alciphron was wrong in suggesting that a μισθωτός could be put to death by his employer. κρεμᾶσθαι, however, probably refers to 'hanging up to be whipped' rather than 'hanging by the neck until dead' (cf. μαστιγούμενον in *D&C* 4.9.1),[53] and in both Longus and Alciphron the simple characters exaggerate their plight in a naive and gently amusing way. In Alciphron Eunape's prediction also suggests what a fierce and vengeful man her husband is.

On any reckoning the case for borrowing by Alciphron from Longus or vice versa is not very strong, but different readers will assess the cumulative weight of the above passages differently and so I append a brief survey of the evidence as to the date of Alciphron.

It is now generally agreed that the case for imitation of Lucian by Alciphron is overwhelmingly strong,[54] but we cannot tell how widely separated in time they may be. That three centuries (?) after Lucian Aristaenetus composed an imaginary correspondence between Lucian and Alciphron (Aristaen. 1.5) tells us nothing. There is virtually no internal evidence to be derived from the *Letters* themselves, as they are for the most part set very firmly in the world of fourth-century B.C. Athens and of the New Comedy.[55] We must therefore fall back again on an argument for literary dependence, this time for borrowings by Aelian (A.D. *c.* 170–230) from Alciphron.[56]

Of the thirty-one names of rustics which appear in the *Letters of farmers* ascribed to Aelian eight also occur in Alciphron; only two are, however, in any way remarkable, Κωμαρχίδης (Alc. 2.29, Aelian 2) and Ἀνθεμίων (Alc. 3.25,

Aelian 4), and of these the former occurs already in Aristophanes (*Peace* 1142) and the latter, in itself not an uncommon name in literature (cf. Pape–Benseler, *Wörterbuch der griechischen Eigennamen s.v.*), may derive in Aelian, as Benner and Fobes point out, from στέφανον ἀνθέμων at Ar. *Ach.* 992 as Epistle 4 is based on *Ach.* 995–8. The parallel passages from the two authors which deserve special mention are as follows: (i) At 2.18.2 and 3.34.3 Alciphron uses the old Attic word φελλεύς, the classical meaning of which seems to have been 'a stony patch of ground fit only for goats'.[57] Aelian's second epistle begins Ἡμέρων ὁ μαλακὸς † φελλέα [M: φελλέαι A: φυλλέα S] διέκοψε [ἐπέκοψε SA] τὸ σκέλος πάνυ χρηστῶς.[58] Benner–Fobes and Leone accept Hercher's φελλεῖ which would here have to mean 'a stone', but it is hard to believe that Aelian would use this word in such a way. As this letter imitates Men. *Georgos* 46ff., Kaibel[59] suggested δικέλληι from *Georgos* 65, but ⟨ἐν τῶι⟩ φελλεῖ is perhaps at least as likely. Whatever the truth, it would be clearly unwise to put too much weight upon these passages. (ii) Alc. 3.5.2 θρύπτεται καὶ συνεχῶς ἀκκίζεται is matched by Aelian 9 ἀκκίζονται [M: ἀκκίζουσι cett.] καὶ θρύπτουσιν ἑαυτάς [θρύπτονται Hercher]. It seems very likely that a lost comic (?) verse lies behind these phrases, but the parallel remains striking, although a very similar phrase in Aelian 1, ἐθρύπτετο καὶ ὡραϊζομένη κτλ., is probably an echo of Eupolis fr. 358 K ὡραϊζομένη καὶ θρυπτομένη (and cf. ὡραΐζονται in Aelian 9). In these same two letters ἀποκλείουσι συνεχῶς in Aelian is matched by συνεχῶς ἀκκίζεται in Alciphron, and there is here a relatively strong case for literary dependence. I can, however, see no convincing grounds for establishing priority, although it might be suggested that Aelian's θρύπτουσιν ἑαυτάς instead of θρύπτονται is a learned Atticism more likely to have been introduced by the later of the two writers.[60] (iii) Alc. 2.34.3 τῶι δὲ ἐγκανάξας κύλικα εὐμεγέθη φλυαρίας φάρμακον ὤρεγον, ὁ δὲ καὶ ταύτην καὶ πλείονας ἐπὶ ταύτηι καὶ ἀδροτέρας ἐκπιὼν οὐκ ἐπαύσατο τῆς ἀδολεσχίας is paralleled by Aelian 4, τρεῖς ἀδρὰς ἐξεκάναξα κύλικας. The verb ἐγκανάσσειν occurs elsewhere only at Ar. *Knights* 105 and ἐκκανάσσειν only in a quotation by Pollux from Eupolis (fr. 272 K).[61] Both writers may independently be showing off their knowledge of a gloss from Old Comedy, but the coincidence of ἁδρός with a compound of this rare verb suggests rather a literary borrowing from one to the other. I see no way to determine the borrower. (iv) Alc. 1.12.1 αἰσχύνεσθαι κορικῶς corresponds to Aelian 19 αἰδουμένη κορικῶς; it is clear that no weight can be put upon this similarity and κορικῶς is used by Aelian elsewhere.[62] In conclusion I think there are sufficient grounds for suspecting that Aelian has occasionally borrowed a phrase from Alciphron or vice versa, but further than that we cannot go.[63]

I suspect that this rather disappointingly inconclusive survey has not provided any good reason to doubt the *communis opinio* that *D&C* was composed in the late second or early third century of our era, and it will be clear from the following chapters that such a dating also suits the novel's literary and stylistic affiliations. Although no startingly novel hypothesis has emerged, I hope that the limits of confidence have now been more clearly defined.

CHAPTER TWO

THE CONSTITUENT ELEMENTS

Even the most casual reader cannot fail to notice that Longus constantly invites us to read his novel at more than one level; almost any passage points the reader in more than one direction, and it has been a major concern of recent Longan scholarship to establish whether any one direction takes precedence over the others or imposes a coherent and consistent pattern on the novel. In this chapter I wish to explore certain aspects of *D&C* with particular attention not to coherent patterns but rather to the novel's ambiguities and open-endedness.

(i) *Daphnis & Chloe*

It has long been recognised that Longus has blurred the status of Daphnis and Chloe so that we are unsure whether to regard them as human or divine.[1] Although it was not uncommon both in real life and on the comic stage for children to be exposed at birth, it is virtually only in myth that they are saved and suckled by animals, and many ancient cultures had stories of gods and the children of gods who were reared in this way.[2] In particular, given the debt of the story to formal drama (cf. below pp. 67–70), Longus may have remembered Euripides' heroine Melanippe whose twin sons by Poseidon were suckled by a cow.[3] Daphnis himself points out that Zeus also was suckled by a goat,[4] and he then proceeds in the same chapter to compare himself first to Pan and then to Dionysus (1.16.3–4); the general similarities between Daphnis and Pan are indeed too striking for any reader to miss. Like the young Zeus in Callimachus' first hymn (vv. 55–6), Daphnis and Chloe ταχὺ μάλα ηὔξησε, καὶ κάλλος αὐτοῖς ἐνεφαίνετο κρεῖττον ἀγροικίας (1.7.1).[5] The names of the children too are ambiguous: Δάφνις was the name of a semi-divine oxherd of mythology (cf. section (ii) below) and Χλόη, apart from the word's general associations with springtime and new growth, was a cult name of Demeter.[6] This name had, however, long ago acquired a purely secular status and it appears in four of Horace's amatory odes (*C.* 1.23, 3.7, 3.9, 3.26). The names of the children's adopted parents, moreover, offer no consistent pattern of meaning: Λάμων occurs as the name of a gardener in a late epigram (*AP* 6.102 = *GP* 2741)[7] and Μυρτάλη is a very common name, as myrtle from its association with Aphrodite often occurs as an element in female names.[8] Νάπη ('glen') is a suitably bucolic name and occurs earlier in literature as the name of an *ancilla* in Ovid (*Am.* 1.11–12). Longus wishes us to remember, however, that Νάπη was, as Strabo 9.426 informs us, the name of a place in the plain of Methymna, and this deepens the sense that we are reading a local μῦθος or aetiological tale. It may also be relevant that Ναπαῖος was an epithet of Apollo on Lesbos (Macrobius, *Sat.* 1.17.45).[9] Significant also is the name of Chloe's adopted father, Δρύας ('oak').

Δρύας is a not uncommon name for mythological characters,[10] and it is possibly significant that it was the name of the father of Lycurgus, one of the traditional opponents and victims of Dionysus (cf. *D&C* 4.3.2); it is perhaps also relevant that, according to one version, Pan's grandfather was called Δρύοψ (*h.Pan* 34). One further occurrence of the name is of particular interest: a papyrus of the third century A.D. (*PSI* 1220) preserves a fragment of a prose narrative of a familiar type, but one in which the characters are given 'meaningful names' of Dionysiac colouring. The text relates how a woman called Hippotis decided not to expose her son, Staphylus ('grapes'), but gave him instead to the Ampeloi ('vines') and then went off to Sardis. The guardian of the Ampeloi gave the child to Dryas the king, who appears to have been the child's real father, and Staphylus is then brought up in the palace ὡς νεώτερος βασιλεύς. Although the story told in this text is of a familiar kind, the unusual names of the characters lend it a very distinctive flavour, and

17

we would like to know more about this fragment of uncertain genre.[11] We can, however, see that the name Δρύας might have had literary and mythological associations for an ancient reader which are lost to us today, and I would also suggest that Longus has perpetrated a literary joke with this name. In the *Iliad* Nestor includes the lapith Dryas in a catalogue of great heroes of the past and gives him the formulaic description ποιμένα λαῶν (1.263); by making his Dryas a real ποιμήν (cf. 1.4.1) Longus provides an added pleasure for those readers who remember the Homeric Δρύας.

The common denominator in many of these names is the element of vegetation and natural growth: Δάφνις ('laurel') and Δρύας ('oak') share a bed in 3.9.5 in a very amusing version of what Achilles Tatius would call a γάμος φυτῶν (cf. Ach. Tat. 1.17.5).[12] The link between the children's experiences and the growth of love on one hand and the continual round of nature and the seasons on the other is now a critical commonplace,[13] but it is more doubtful whether we should also see in Daphnis and Chloe 'Year Spirits' whose passion is enacted in the novel: great care is needed when labelling a phrase or expression 'mystical'. Thus, for example, when the snows of winter keep them apart the children 'waited for spring as a rebirth from death' (ἐκ θανάτου παλιγγενεσίαν, 3.4.2). This phrase perhaps recalls the mystery religions more strongly than any other in the work, and yet the idea that winter is death seems to us 'natural', and Horace at least is one poet who fully exploits this link (cf. C. 1.4, 1.9, 4.7).[14] Closer in time to *D&C* is probably the opening of the anonymous *Peruigilium Veneris*:

> uer nouum, uer iam canorum: uere natus orbis est.
> uere concordant amores, uere nubunt alites.   (vv. 2-3)

Although the text of v. 2 is not certain,[15] the idea of the rebirth of the world in spring must be present in this couplet; editors note that the Stoics seem to have placed the birth of the world in springtime (Chrysippus fr. 584, *SVF* II p. 180) and they compare Virgil's lines on the infancy of the earth:

non alios prima crescentis origine mundi
inluxisse dies aliumue habuisse tenorem
crediderim: uer illud erat, uer magnus agebat
orbis et hibernis parcebant flatibus Euri,
cum primae lucem pecudes hausere, uirumque
terrea progenies duris caput extulit aruis,
immissaeque ferae siluis et sidera caelo.
nec res hunc tenerae possent perferre laborem,
si non tanta quies iret frigusque caloremque
inter, et exciperet caeli indulgentia terras.

(*Georg.* 2.336–45)

The description of the seasons was a standard exercise in the rhetorical schools[16] and it seems a small step from Libanius' image of winter as a prison (λύει [sc. τὸ ἦρ] ὥσπερ ἐκ δεσμωτηρίου τοὺς ἀνθρώπους τοῦ χειμῶνος, 8.479–80 F) to the notion of spring as rebirth from death. Like so much else in the work, this phrase suggests more than one layer of meaning, and it is this playful richness which is perhaps the most attractive feature of the novel.

Not only do Daphnis and Chloe resemble the gods but, like nature itself, they repeat their cycle of experience with their own children (4.39.2). On a different level they often resemble the animals they care for, cf. 1.10.3 θᾶττον ἄν τις εἶδε τὰ ποιμνία καὶ τὰς αἶγας ἀπ' ἀλλήλων μεμερισμένας ἢ Χλόην καὶ Δάφνιν, 2.38.2 αἵ τε αἶγες πλησίον τῶν προβάτων ἤιεσαν ὅ τε Δάφνις ἐβάδιζεν ἐγγὺς τῆς Χλόης. Nevertheless, they remain recognisably human, and a dictum of Aristotle about the difference between men and animals applies with particular force to them: τό τε ... μιμεῖσθαι σύμφυτον τοῖς ἀνθρώποις ἐκ παίδων ἐστὶ καὶ τούτωι διαφέρουσι τῶν ἄλλων ζώιων ὅτι μιμητικώτατόν ἐστι καὶ τὰς μαθήσεις ποιεῖται διὰ μιμήσεως τὰς πρώτας, καὶ τὸ χαίρειν τοῖς μιμήμασι πάντας (*Poetics* 1448b5–9). This difference between the human and the animal world is much exploited by Longus.[17] The first time that we encounter animals in the novel they are caring for the foundlings to the neglect of their own offspring (1.2.1, 1.5.1). This is in pointed contrast to civilised man who, as we learn in the fourth book, exposes his children to the caprices of nature; even Lamon has at first the unworthy

19

intention of taking only the recognition tokens and leaving Daphnis to die (1.3.1). Nobler thoughts, however, get the better of him as he feels ashamed εἰ μηδὲ αἰγὸς φιλανθρωπίαν μιμήσεται. Daphnis and Chloe also learn to sing, dance and gather flowers by imitation of the birds, the lambs and the bees (1.9.2). For only one activity, that of lovemaking, is such an education insufficient – here τέχνη is needed to bring natural desires to fulfilment, cf. 1.17.1: Chloe's kiss is ἀδίδακτον καὶ ἄτεχνον, 3.18.1: Daphnis begs Lycaenion ὅτι τάχιστα διδάξαι τὴν τέχνην δι' ἧς ὃ βούλεται δράσει Χλόην.[18] In this respect Daphnis and Chloe well illustrate another of Aristotle's dicta, ὅλως τε ἡ τέχνη τὰ μὲν ἐπιτελεῖ ἃ ἡ φύσις ἀδυνατεῖ ἀπεργάσασθαι, τὰ δὲ μιμεῖται (Physics 2.199a15). The children conform to a common ancient conception of the life of primitive man in the Golden Age: man, who was originally ἄτεχνος,[19] developed skills and arts by imitating the natural world,[20] and Chloe's arguments for imitating the lovemaking of sheep and goats at 3.14.4 thus produce one of the nicest ironies in the work. How close are the links between the traditional picture of the rustic Golden Age and the life of Daphnis and Chloe may be gauged from the following passage of Propertius:[21]

> felix agrestum quondam pacata iuuentus,
>   diuitiae quorum messis et arbor erant!
> illis munus erant decussa Cydonia ramo,
>   et dare puniceis plena canistra rubis,
> nunc uiolas tondere manu, nunc mixta referre
>   lilia uimineos lucida per calathos,
> et portare suis uestitas frondibus uuas
>   aut uariam plumae uersicoloris auem.
> his tum blanditiis furtiua per antra puellae
>   oscula siluicolis empta dedere uiris.
> hinnulei pellis totos operibat amantis,
>   altaque natiuo creuerat herba toro,
> pinus et incumbens lentas circumdabat umbras;
>   nec fuerat nudas poena uidere deas;
> corniger Idaei uacuam pastoris in aulam
>   dux aries saturas ipse reduxit ouis;
> dique deaeque omnes, quibus est tutela per agros,
>   praebebant uestri uerba benigna foci:

'Et leporem, quicumque uenis, uenaberis, hospes,
   et si forte meo tramite quaeris auem:
et me Pana tibi comitem de rupe uocato,
   siue petes calamo praemia, siue cane.'

(Prop. 3.13.25–46)

The idea of the Golden Age was important in the second
century, but we must not overstress its role in D&C: although
it is true that the peasant farmer was often seen as the last
survivor of the Golden Age[22] and the character of Gnathon
clearly besmirches the pristine purity of the countryside
(cf. below pp. 70–1), the life of Daphnis and Chloe is idyllic
largely because they are young; life is not always easy for
their foster-parents (cf. 3.30.3). If we sense that Daphnis and
Chloe are never going to find life difficult, this is partly
because of their piety and their devotion to each other (cf.
4.39.1), but partly also because they are to be incorporated,
at least partially, into the polite, urban society of Dionysophanes and Astylus and never fully experience how hard it is
to survive in the countryside.

The life of Daphnis and Chloe and the landscape which
they inhabit have a quite different tone from the poetry of
Theocritus to whom Longus owes his largest literary debt (cf.
below pp. 59–63). I have already noted a certain affinity
between D&C and the poetry of Tibullus (above pp. 5–6), but
the closest Greek analogues are probably to be found in the
Acharnians and Peace of Aristophanes, which share with
Tibullus and Longus an opposition between the unpleasant-
ness of war and a quiet and happy life in the countryside.
In comparison with Theocritus, all three writers clearly
present an idealised picture of life in the countryside. The
modern study of ancient bucolic literature has, however,
been too concerned to label a given landscape or individual
detail as 'realistic' or 'idyllic' where very often no such
simple division is possible. There are many different shades
of 'reality'. There is very little natural description in D&C
which it is hard to believe in as being a view of Lesbos, even
if there is also little which must be Lesbos and nowhere else.
The landscape is generalised but not meaningless.[23] It may be

21

termed 'idyllic' in that we are given only a partial view, and Longus' selection of natural features is much more limited than that of Theocritus,[24] but it is not pure fantasy. A helpful comparison may be drawn from the description of the seasons. In *D&C* all of the seasons are painted in their strongest colours: budding spring (1.9, 3.12–13), burning summer (1.23, 3.24), rich autumn (2.1, 4.1), freezing winter (3.3). All of these are 'realistic' in the sense that the seasons can be like this (even if winter on Lesbos is only rarely very fierce), but they are also fashioned to conform to our preconceived notions and expectations (particularly as these are drawn from the literary and rhetorical traditions). Much the same could be said of Longus' descriptions of the vintage and indeed the whole of his account of life in the countryside.

(ii) *The legend of Daphnis*

By the later Hellenistic period the name Δάφνις had developed from being that of a mythical βουκόλος, whose erotic ἄλγεα were the subject *par excellence* of 'bucolic' song and who was himself, according to some versions, the πρῶτος εὑρετής of bucolic poetry, into the name of any typical shepherd. Already in the Theocritean corpus we find characters called Daphnis who have only some or indeed none of the features of the legendary hero (cf. *Idylls* 8, 9, 27). Longus therefore need not have had the legendary Daphnis in mind when he gave this name to his leading character, but it is clear that he has in fact used certain features of the legend in his story. There is much here that is familiar and requires little comment, but the most recent treatment of this subject, that of Wojaczek ([1969] 5–21), is so vitiated by error and rash assumption that a new survey will not be out of place. I have not included in this survey those places where Longus has echoed a passage of Theocritus concerning the legendary Daphnis merely for ornamental effect (cf. below p. 59); as an example of such passages 1.18.2 may serve: οἶον ἀκμάζει τὰ ἄνθη, κἀγὼ στεφάνους οὐ πλέκω, ἀλλὰ τὰ μὲν ἴα καὶ ὁ ὑάκινθος ἀνθεῖ, Δάφνις δὲ μαραίνεται, where we inevitably think of the 'wasting of Daphnis' in Theocritus, *Idyll* 1.

Our main sources for the legend of Daphnis are reports in Diodorus Siculus (4.84), Aelian (*VH* 10.18) and Parthenius (*Erot.Path.*29 = *FGrH* 566 F83) and the accounts given by the ancient commentators on Theocritus and on the *Eclogues* of Virgil. It is particularly unfortunate that we do not know more of the Δαφνιακά of the Byzantine poet and historian Agathias: in a surviving epigram (*AP* 6.80 = 4 Viansino, quoted on p. 41 below) Agathias dedicates the nine books of the Δαφνιακά to Aphrodite, and from Agathias' *Histories* we learn that the Δαφνιακά consisted of ἐν ἑξαμέτροις βραχέα ἄττα ποιήματα . . . μύθοις τισὶ πεποικιλμένα ἐρωτικοῖς καὶ τῶν τοιούτων ἀναπλέα γοητευμάτων (*Proem* 7). If this work had survived it might have shed considerable light upon *D&C*.

In broad outline the tale told by our sources is that Daphnis was the child of Hermes and a nymph and was exposed in the open, found and reared by nymphs (or, in other versions, shepherds), became an oxherd and a wonderful singer and was himself loved by a nymph. He promised the nymph that he would have nothing to do with any other girl and when he broke his promise, either voluntarily, or according to some reports, under the influence of alcohol, the nymph deprived him of his eyesight.

According to Diodorus, Daphnis was exposed by his mother in a *locus amoenus* around a grove sacred to the Nymphs; in Longus, Chloe is found in a cave of the Nymphs and the children have a special relationship with these divinities. The divine status of the legendary Daphnis is matched by the supernatural protection which the children receive after they have been exposed, but a major difference is that whereas the Daphnis of mythology was ὁ βουκόλος *par excellence*, Longus' Daphnis is put in charge of the goats. In the rustic hierarchy which we find in literature goatherds were at the bottom and oxherds at the top of the social ladder (cf. Donatus, *Vita Verg.* 49 = Wendel, *Prolegomena* p. 17), but Longus' choice of occupation for Daphnis

had as much to do with sex as with social status. In the first
idyll of Theocritus Priapus addresses the dying Daphnis thus:

> Δάφνι τάλαν, τί τὺ τάκεαι; ἁ δέ τυ κώρα
> πάσας ἀνὰ κράνας, πάντ᾽ ἄλσεα ποσσὶ φορεῖται –
> ἄρχετε βουκολικᾶς, Μοῖσαι φίλαι, ἄρχετ᾽ ἀοιδᾶς –
> ζάτεισ᾽. ἆ δύσερώς τις ἄγαν καὶ ἀμήχανος ἐσσί.
> βούτας μὲν ἐλέγευ, νῦν δ᾽ αἰπόλωι ἀνδρὶ ἔοικας.
> ᾡπόλος, ὅκκ᾽ ἐσορῆι τὰς μηκάδας οἷα βατεῦνται,
> τάκεται ὀφθαλμὼς ὅτι οὐ τράγος αὐτὸς ἔγεντο.

(Theocr. 1.82–8)

Modern critics have concluded from a combination of this
passage, Theocr. 6.6–7 βάλλει τοι, Πολύφαμε, τὸ ποίμνιον
ἁ Γαλάτεια | μάλοισιν, δυσέρωτα καὶ [Meineke: τὸν codd.]
αἰπόλον ἄνδρα καλεῦσα, and D&C 3.18.1 ὁ Δάφνις ... ἅτε
ἄγροικος καὶ αἰπόλος καὶ ἐρῶν καὶ νέος ... τὴν Λυκαίνιον
ἱκέτευεν ὅτι τάχιστα διδάξαι τὴν τέχνην, δι᾽ ἧς ὃ βούλεται
δράσει Χλόην, that goatherds were traditionally unlucky
or inexperienced in love,[25] but it is noteworthy that at
least one scholiast interpreted Theocr. 1.86 in quite the
opposite way: βούτας μὲν ἐλέγευ · βουκόλος ὤν, φησίν,
οὐ κατὰ βουκόλους ἐρᾶις. οἱ μὲν γὰρ βουκόλοι πρὸς τὴν
τῶν ἀφροδισίων μῖξιν ἐγκρατεῖς, τοὐναντιόν δὲ λαγνότατοι
οἱ αἰπόλοι. καὶ ἡ αἰτία, ὅτι κατωφερέστεραι οὖσαι αἱ αἶγες
δελεάζουσι τοὺς αἰπόλους. Longus, too, has exploited to
the full the humorous possibilities of associating his naive
and (unhappily) innocent hero with animals which were
notoriously randy and smelly (cf. 1.16.3, 1.18.1, 3.14.4,
4.11.2). By making Daphnis a goatherd Longus also makes
particularly pointed the similarity between Daphnis and
Pan: when Daphnis tries unsuccessfully to mount Chloe
μιμούμενος τοὺς τράγους (3.14.5) we are reminded of Pan's
greater success with she-goats which is commemorated in
the epithet αἰγιβάτης. What follows, ἔκλαεν [sc. ὁ Δάφνις]
εἰ καὶ κριῶν ἀμαθέστερος εἰς τὰ ἔρωτος ἔργα, not only
reworks the idea of Theocr. 1.87–8 (quoted above) but also
humorously expresses Daphnis' sense of the superiority
of τράγοι to κριοί. The notion of Daphnis as a τράγος is
exploited with a fine touch in 1.12 in which Daphnis falls

24

into a pit together with a τράγος and both are pulled out by Chloe and Dorcon.

It is possible also that in creating the character of Daphnis Longus was influenced by the figure of Κομάτας in Theocritus' Seventh Idyll. In this poem the mysterious Lycidas sings a song in which he imagines the party that he will hold to celebrate the safe arrival of his beloved Ageanax in Mytilene (a destination which provides one link between this poem and *D&C*):

αὐλησεῦντι δέ μοι δύο ποιμένες, εἷς μὲν Ἀχαρνεύς,
εἷς δὲ Λυκωπίτας· ὁ δὲ Τίτυρος ἐγγύθεν ἀισεῖ
ὡς ποκα τᾶς Ξενέας ἠράσσατο Δάφνις ὁ βούτας,
χὡς ὄρος ἀμφεπονεῖτο καὶ ὡς δρύες αὐτὸν ἐθρήνευν
Ἱμέρα αἵτε φύοντι παρ' ὄχθαισιν ποταμοῖο,
εὖτε χιὼν ὥς τις κατετάκετο μακρὸν ὑφ' Αἷμον
ἢ Ἄθω ἢ Ῥοδόπαν ἢ Καύκασον ἐσχατόωντα.
ἀισεῖ δ' ὥς ποκ' ἔδεκτο τὸν αἰπόλον εὐρέα λάρναξ
ζωὸν ἐόντα κακαῖσιν ἀτασθαλίαισιν ἄνακτος,
ὥς τέ νιν αἱ σιμαὶ λειμωνόθε φέρβον ἰοῖσαι
κέδρον ἐς ἀδεῖαν μαλακοῖς ἄνθεσσι μέλισσαι,
οὕνεκά οἱ γλυκὺ Μοῖσα κατὰ στόματος χέε νέκταρ.
ὢ μακαριστὲ Κομᾶτα, τύ θην τάδε τερπνὰ πεπόνθεις·
καὶ τὺ κατεκλάισθης ἐς λάρνακα, καὶ τὺ μελισσᾶν
κηρία φερβόμενος ἔτος ὥριον ἐξεπόνασας.
αἴθ' ἐπ' ἐμεῦ ζωοῖς ἐναρίθμιος ὤφελες ἦμεν
ὥς τοι ἐγὼν ἐνόμευον ἀν' ὤρεα τὰς καλὰς αἶγας
φωνᾶς εἰσαίων, τὺ δ' ὑπὸ δρυσὶν ἢ ὑπὸ πεύκαις
ἀδὺ μελισδόμενος κατεκέκλισο, θεῖε Κομᾶτα.'

(Theocr. 7.71–89)

It is clear from the scholia to this passage that ancient scholars identified Comatas as the goatherd who was fed by bees when he was shut in a chest, despite the problematic καὶ τύ of v. 84 which continues to puzzle editors of Theocritus. In *Idyll 5* also, Comatas is the name of a goatherd, and the scholiast on *Syrinx* 1–3, Οὐδενὸς εὐνάτειρα Μακροπτολέμοιο δὲ μάτηρ|μαίας ἀντιπέτροιο θοὸν τέκεν ἰθυντῆρα, |οὐχὶ Κεράσταν ὅν ποτε θρέψατο ταυροπάτωρ, explains v. 3 of that poem as a reference to the goatherd Comatas who was fed by bees (cf. Gow ad loc.). Beyond these references, however, ancient scholars knew nothing

25

about Comatas, but as it is clear from *Idyll* 7 that Comatas was a legendary bucolic singer and as scholars knew that Daphnis had been exposed by his mother (Σ Theocr. 7.78–9) and also that in some versions he had been nourished by bees (Σ Theocr. 7.83), they thought that Theocritus must have transferred some features of the legend of Daphnis to his account of Comatas and even that *Syrinx* 3, οὐχὶ Κεράσταν ὅν ποτε θρέψατο ταυροπάτωρ, referred not to Comatas but to Daphnis.[26] In seeking to explain Theocritus' account, the scholia cite from Lycus of Rhegium (*FGrH* 570 F7) the story of a nameless shepherd or goatherd who was locked by his king into a chest but was saved by the Muses who fed him on honeycombs, and most modern scholars assume that the character in Lycus' story was already known as Comatas before Theocritus; although this is indeed quite likely, it would be rash to assume it to be true, if only because Theocritus is here almost certainly using earlier, now lost, poetry and may be combining his sources in such a way as to produce a quite new μῦθος. It will be sufficient, therefore, to note that Longus may have been thinking of the exposure and wondrous nurture of Comatas in *Idyll* 7 as well as of the better-known story of Daphnis.[27]

An epigram by 'Zonas of Sardis' (*AP* 9.556 = *GP* 3486–91)[28] is an address by Pan to the nymphs:

Νύμφαι ἐποχθίδιαι Νηρηίδες, εἴδετε Δάφνιν
χθιζόν, ἐπαχνιδίαν ὡς ἀπέλουσε κόμαν,
ὑμετέραις λιβάδεσσιν ὅτ' ἔνθορε σειριόκαυτος
ἠρέμα φοινιχθεὶς μᾶλα παρηίδια;
εἴπατέ μοι, καλὸς ἦν; ἢ ἐγὼ τράγος οὐκ ἄρα κνάμαν
μοῦνον ἐγυιώθην, ἀλλ' ἔτι καὶ κραδίαν;

This poem, which probably derives from the first century B.C., reminds us of the scene in *D&C* in which Daphnis washes himself in the νυμφαῖον and the sight of his naked flesh arouses desire in Chloe (1.13–14). A work of art is a not unlikely source of inspiration for Zonas' epigram: Pan as ἐραστής of Daphnis is familiar from both literature and art, and bathing is a very common motif in ancient painting.[29] In any event, the poem suggests that Longus was following an earlier tradition in connection with Daphnis' bath. Bathing is, of course, an obvious motif in an erotic context and particularly to be noted is the scene at Chariton 2.2.2 where Callirhoe is washed: Longus' description, τὰ νῶτα δὲ ἀπολουούσης ἡ σάρξ ὑπέπιπτε μαλθακή, ὥστε λαθοῦσα ἑαυτῆς ἥψατο πολλάκις, εἰ τρυφερώτερος [Geel: -τέρα] εἴη πειρωμένη, is closely paralleled by Chariton's, ὁ χρὼς γὰρ λευκὸς ἔστιλψεν εὐθὺς μαρμαρυγῆι τινι ὅμοιον ἀπολάμπων· τρυφερὰ δὲ σάρξ, ὥστε δεδοικέναι μὴ καὶ ἡ τῶν δακτύλων ἐπαφὴ μέγα τραῦμα ποιήσηι. (By way of contrast, the description of Chloe's bath (1.32.1) is far less sensual.) In short, Longus' debt to the traditional legend of Daphnis in the bathing scene should not be overstated. Here may also conveniently be mentioned 4.4.1, τὸν Διόνυσον ἐστεφάνωσε, τοῖς ἄνθεσιν ὕδωρ ἐπωχέτευσεν ἐκ πηγῆς τινὸς ἣν εὗρεν ἐς τὰ ἄνθη Δάφνις · ἐσχόλαζε μὲν τοῖς ἄνθεσιν ἡ πηγή, Δάφνιδος δὲ ὅμως ἐκαλεῖτο πηγή. This curiously loose (and very curiously worded) detail in the description of Lamon's garden may be related to the information supplied by Servius (on Ecl. 5.20) that after the blinding of Daphnis Mercury carried his son up into heaven and that on the spot from where Daphnis had disappeared the god caused the spring called 'Daphnis' to arise; at this spring the Sicilians held annual sacrifices. Here Longus has apparently integrated into his story a detail from the original myth with less than his usual skill.

The oath of undying affection which Daphnis and Chloe swear to each other in 2.39 may recall the oath of fidelity which Daphnis swears to the nymph in the common version of the Sicilian legend, but Longus here also has his eye on purely literary models. We are reminded of the oath which the young cowherd swears to his girl in Theocritus, Idyll 27, ὄμνυε μὴ μετὰ λέκτρα λιπὼν ἀέκουσαν ἀπενθεῖν. |:: οὐ μαυτὸν τὸν Πᾶνα καὶ ἢν ἐθέλῃς με διώξαι (vv. 35-6) and also of Catullus' Acme and Septimius:

Acmen Septimius suos amores
tenens in gremio 'mea' inquit 'Acme,
ni te perdite amo atque amare porro

27

omnes sum assidue paratus annos,
quantum qui pote plurimum perire,
solus in Libya Indiaque tosta
caesio ueniam obuius leoni.'
hoc ut dixit, Amor sinistra ut ante
dextra sternuit approbationem.
at Acme leuiter caput reflectens
et dulcis pueri ebrios ocellos
illo purpureo ore suauiata,
'sic', inquit 'mea uita Septimille,
huic uni domino usque seruiamus,
ut multo mihi maior acriorque
ignis mollibus ardet in medullis.'
hoc ut dixit, Amor sinistra ut ante
dextra sternuit approbationem.
nunc ab auspicio bono profecti
mutuis animis amant amantur.
unam Septimius misellus Acmen
mauult quam Syrias Britanniasque:
uno in Septimio fidelis Acme
facit delicias libidinesque.
quis ullos homines beatiores
uidit, quis Venerem auspicatiorem?   (Catullus 45)

It seems very likely that behind both Catullus and Longus
and the use of this motif in the novel in general[30] lies lost
Hellenistic erotic poetry; where Catullus and Longus stand
out is that they celebrate the power and firmness of lovers'
oaths, whereas it is more usual to find poets complaining
about how little value such oaths have.

A further link with the traditional story of Daphnis may
be Chromis' wife,[31] Lycaenion, who seduces Daphnis in
3.15–18, (for the implication of this woman's name cf. below
p. 68). One version of Philargyrius' note on *Ecl.* 5.20
names the nymph who loved Daphnis as *Lyca uel Hedina*,
and so Longus may have been aware of an association
between Daphnis and a lady with a Λυκ- name. It is, however,
equally likely that this is simply a coincidence; in the extant
versions of the legends of Daphnis a large variety of names is
given to the woman in his life.[32]

Some versions of the legend report that, after he had been
blinded, Daphnis fell over a cliff or was turned into a large

rock in the shape of a man or suffered some combination of these two incidents.[33] Longus may be thinking of this story in 4.22 where Daphnis is about to throw himself off a cliff as he sees Astylus chasing him, but he is also certainly aware of Theocr. 3.25 τὰν βαίταν ἀποδὺς ἐς κύματα τηνῶ ἀλεῦμαι and 5.15-6 ἢ κατὰ τήνας|τᾶς πέτρας ... μανεὶς εἰς Κρᾶθιν ἀλοίμαν. A further influence here might have been the legend, attested most notably in a fragment of Menander's Λευκαδία (fr. 258 K–T), of the leap of the lovesick Sappho from the Leucadian rock.[34] The Lesbian setting of the novel allows Longus to make pointed use of the poetry of Sappho (cf. below pp. 73–6) and may indeed partly have been dictated by this possibility. Like many other allusions in the novel, however, this reference remains in the background and is not laboured or thrust harshly before us.

After Daphnis has been recognised by his parents he collects his equipment and dedicates it to the gods, τῶι Διονύσωι μὲν ἀνέθηκε τὴν πήραν καὶ τὸ δέρμα, τῶι Πανὶ τὴν σύριγγα καὶ τὸν πλάγιον αὐλόν, τὴν καλαύροπα ταῖς Νύμφαις καὶ τοὺς γαυλοὺς οὓς αὐτὸς ἐτεκτήνατο (4.26.2). In two late epigrams a shepherd called Daphnis dedicates his gear (AP 6.73, 6.78)[35] but Longus is here primarily thinking of Theocritus, Epigr. 2 Gow (AP 6.177):

Δάφνις ὁ λευκόχρως, ὁ καλᾶι σύριγγι μελίσδων
βουκολικοὺς ὕμνους, ἄνθετο Πανὶ τάδε,
τοὺς τρητοὺς δόνακας, τὸ λαγωβόλον, ὀξὺν ἄκοντα,
νεβρίδα, τὰν πήραν ᾆ ποκ' ἐμαλοφόρει.

Although there are elements of the legendary Daphnis in this poem (cf. vv. 1–2), this character is really no more than a typical shepherd,[36] and this dedication corresponds to no part of the myth of Daphnis as our main sources tell it. In this connection we would like to know more of a poem by Lycophronides (?fourth century B.C.) from which Clearchus cited a fragment in his Ἐρωτικά (apud Ath. 15.670e = Clearchus fr. 24 W² = PMG 844):

τόδ' ἀνατίθημί σοι Ῥόδον
καλὸν Ῥνόημα, καὶ πέδιλα καὶ κυνέαν
καὶ τὰν θηροφόνον λογχίδ', ἐπεί μοι νόος ἄλλαι κέχυται
ἐπὶ τὰν Χάρισιν φίλαν παῖδα καὶ καλάν.

According to Clearchus–Athenaeus the speaker is an αἰπόλος
ἐρῶν and we may conjecture that σοι in v.
1 is most probably
Pan, but without more information we can go no further in
assessing the possible influence of this poem on Longus.
Longus, however, uses the dedication, as it was used so often
in both life and literature, as a sign of the abandonment of
one sort of life for another rather than as a sign of love-
sickness.

Finally, I return to 4.15 which was considered above in
the context of the relationship between Longus and Alciphron. It has been noted that in a passage of Silius Italicus
the legendary Daphnis is described in terms appropriate to
Orpheus:

> hos inter Daphnis, deductum ab origine nomen
> antiqua, fuit infelix, cui linquere saltus
> et mutare casas infido marmore uisum.
> at princeps generis quanto maiora parauit
> intra pastorem sibi nomina! Daphnin amarunt
> Sicelides Musae; dexter donauit auena
> Phoebus Castalia et iussit, proiectus in herba
> si quando caneret, laetos per prata, per arua
> ad Daphnin properare greges riuosque silere.
> ille ubi, septena modulatus harundine carmen,
> mulcebat siluas, non umquam tempore eodem
> Siren assuetos effudit in aequore cantus;
> Scyllaei tacuere canes; stetit atra Charybdis;
> et laetus scopulis audiuit iubila Cyclops.
> progeniem hauserunt et nomen amabile flammae.

(Sil. Ital. 14.462–76)

Although Wojaczek ([1969] 19–20) makes much of this
passage, which he seems to have misunderstood, it really
tells us no more than that poets chose to describe one famous
musician in terms normally associated with another. What is
important is that both Longus and Alciphron in 2.9 (cf.
above p. 8) are indebted to a rhetorical commonplace and

also to art. Orpheus amid the animals was a very common subject in Roman wall-painting,[37] and Philostratus the Younger describes such a painting in which trees form a θέατρον on which the birds sit to listen to Orpheus (6.2, cf. Longus 4.15.2). Precisely the same conceit is found in a description of a gem at Heliodorus 5.14.3 (a shepherd boy is playing to his flocks) γέγραπτο καὶ ἀρνίων ἀπαλὰ σκιρτήματα καὶ οἱ μὲν ἀγεληδὸν ἐπὶ τὴν πέτραν ἀνατρέχοντες, οἱ δὲ περὶ τὸν νομέα κύκλους ἀγερώχους ἐξελίττοντες ποιμενικὸν θέατρον ἐπεδείκνυσαν τὸν κρημνόν.[38]

It is thus clear that although Longus has peppered his narrative with details from the legend of the Sicilian Daphnis, he has made no effort to use the legend as a constant narrative frame.[39] Such selectivity is typical of him: he drew material from a great many sources, but did not reproduce any one source so faithfully that it came to dominate the narrative.

(iii) *The gods in* Daphnis & Chloe

No aspect of Longus' novel has attracted so much recent comment as his treatment of the divine. Here again we must be wary of trying to force one 'meaning' upon the work: the mention of a god's name will obviously produce different reactions in a layman and in an initiate of that god's mysteries. Similarly, when Dionysophanes exclaims to Megacles ἀμφοτέρους ἐξεθήκαμεν, ἀμφοτέρους εὑρήκαμεν, ἀμφοτέρων ἐμέλησε Πανὶ καὶ Νύμφαις καὶ Ἔρωτι (4.36.2), different readers will give varying weight to the religious solemnity of such an asyndetic formula[40] in the light of Longus' prose style as a whole. My aim in this section is, therefore, simply to sketch some of the background against which any interpretation must be measured.

The god who is clearly in control of the events of the novel is Eros,[41] and in 2.4-7 Philetas presents a lengthy description of this god (cf. below p. 77-8). One day in his garden Philetas saw Eros playing amidst the flowers, a traditional place to find this god (cf. Pl. *Symp.* 196a-b), and when the old man tried to catch him the little god easily slipped away. This passage is replete with material familiar from archaic and Hellenistic erotic poetry, and Eros here is the mischievous child with whom we are all only too well acquainted. When, however, the god addresses Philetas in 2.5.2 he claims to be τοῦ Κρόνου πρεσβύτερος καὶ αὐτοῦ τοῦ παντὸς χρόνου, even though he looks like a child,[42] i.e. he claims to be the cosmogonic Eros of Hesiod (*Theog.* 120), and this is supported by Philetas' description of his powers at 2.7.2:[43]

δύναται δὲ τοσοῦτον ὅσον οὐδὲ ὁ Ζεύς · κρατεῖ μὲν στοιχείων, κρατεῖ δὲ ἄστρων, κρατεῖ δὲ τῶν ὁμοίων θεῶν . . . τὰ ἄνθη πάντα Ἔρωτος ἔργα, τὰ φυτὰ πάντα τούτου ποιήματα, διὰ τοῦτον καὶ ποταμοὶ ῥέουσι καὶ ἄνεμοι πνέουσιν. This passage is, in both content and style, very like other descriptions of 'syncretic monotheisms' (Chalk [1960] 33) of the Hellenistic and imperial periods; Isis' self-presentation at Apuleius, *Met.* 11.5 may serve as a representative example: *en adsum tuis commota, Luci, precibus, rerum naturae parens, elementorum omnium domina,*[44] *saeculorum progenies initialis, summa numinum, regina manium, prima caelitum, deorum dearumque facies uniformis, quae caeli luminosa culmina, maris salubria flamina, inferum deplorata silentia nutibus meis dispenso.* The use of stereotyped language does not, of course, necessarily diminish the religious power of any statement (it often in fact increases it), and the Hesiodic Eros was indeed associated in later antiquity with the set of beliefs which we designate as 'Orphic'.[45] Nevertheless, further positive indications of an 'Orphic' Eros in Longus seem to me to be very scanty,[46] and it is necessary to place 2.4–7 in its proper context. The contrast between Eros' great age and his apparent youth appears first in Socratic literature of the fourth century B.C. (Xen. *Symp.* 8.1, cf. Pl. *Symp.* 195b–c)[47] and the control which this force exerts over the whole of nature is a commonplace of classical poetry, cf. E. *Hipp.* 447–50, 1272–81 (with W. S. Barrett's note on 1277–80), V. *Georg.* 3.242–83. In particular we may be reminded of the proem to Book 1 of Lucretius and of a rather later piece of poetry, the 'Orphic' *Hymn to Eros* (no. 58).

Aeneadum genetrix, hominum diuumque uoluptas,
alma Venus, caeli subter labentia signa
quae mare nauigerum, quae terras frugiferentis
concelebras, per te quoniam genus omne animantum
concipitur uisitque exortum lumina solis:
te, dea, te fugiunt uenti, te nubila caeli
aduentumque tuum, tibi suauis daedala tellus
summittit flores, tibi rident aequora ponti
placatumque nitet diffuso lumine caelum.
nam simul ac species patefactast uerna diei
et reserata uiget genitabilis aura fauoni,
aeriae primum uolucres te, diua, tuumque
significant initum perculsae corda tua ui.
inde ferae pecudes persultant pabula laeta
et rapidos tranant amnis: ita capta lepore
te sequitur cupide quo quamque inducere pergis.
denique per maria ac montis fluuiosque rapaces
frondiferasque domos auium camposque uirentis
omnibus incutiens blandum per pectora amorem
efficis ut cupide generatim saecla propagent.
quae quoniam rerum naturam sola gubernas
nec sine te quicquam dias in luminis oras
exoritur neque fit laetum neque amabile quicquam,
te sociam studeo scribendis uersibus esse
quos ego de rerum natura pangere conor
Memmiadae nostro, quem tu, dea, tempore in omni
omnibus ornatum uoluisti excellere rebus.

(Lucretius 1.1–27)

κικλήσκω μέγαν, ἀγνόν, ἐράσμιον, ἡδὺν Ἔρωτα,
τοξαλκῆ, πτερόεντα, πυρίδρομον, εὔδρομον ὁρμῆι,
συμπαίζοντα θεοῖς ἠδὲ θνητοῖς ἀνθρώποις,
εὐπάλαμον, διφυῆ, πάντων κληῖδας ἔχοντα,
αἰθέρος οὐρανίου, πόντου, χθονός, ἠδ' ὅσα θνητοῖς
πνεύματα παντογένεθλα θεὰ βόσκει χλοόκαρπος,
ἠδ' ὅσα Τάρταρος εὐρὺς ἔχει πόντος θ' ἁλίδουπος·
μοῦνος γὰρ τούτων πάντων οἴηκα κρατύνεις.
ἀλλά, μάκαρ, καθαραῖς γνώμαις μύσταισι συνέρχου,
φαύλους δ' ἐκτοπίους θ' ὁρμὰς ἀπὸ τῶνδ' ἀπόπεμπε.

(Orph. Hymn 58)

The weight of these passages of 'serious' literature[48] is partly offset by the appearance of these themes in other, more playful, contexts. In Lucian's *Dialogues of the gods* Zeus

33

asks Eros, σὺ παίδιον ὁ Ἔρως, ὃς ἀρχαιότερος εἶ πολὺ Ἰαπετοῦ; ἢ διότι μὴ πώγωνα μηδὲ πολιὰς ἔφυσας, διὰ ταῦτα καὶ βρέφος ἀξιοῖς νομίζεσθαι γέρων καὶ πανοῦργος ὤν; (6.1). In similarly amusing vein, the hero of the fragmentary *Romance of Metiochus and Parthenope*[49] derides the traditional picture of Eros: βωμολόχοι μέν, εἶπεν, ... οἱ τῆς ἀληθοῦς παιδείας ἀμύητοι ... μυθολογίαις ἐπακολουθοῦσι, ὡς ἔστιν ὁ Ἔρως Ἀφροδίτης υἱὸς κομιδῆι νέος ἔχω⟨ν πτέρ⟩α καὶ τῶι νώτωι παρηρτημένον τόξον [Diels: παρηρκτημενον δοξον] καὶ ⟨τῆι χειρὶ⟩ κρατῶν λαμπάδα τούτοις τε τοῖς ὅπλοις ... τὰς ψυχὰς τῶν ⟨νέων τιτρώ⟩σκει. γέλως δ᾽ ἂν εἴη τὸ τοιοῦτο πρῶτον ... βρέφος μὴ τελειωθῆναι. The text becomes too broken to make further reproduction worthwhile, but it is clear that Metiochus makes fun of the god who has remained a child ever since time began and allegedly wanders around the world shooting and burning people. The age of a god was in fact a topos of a rhetorical ἐγκώμιον θεοῦ (cf. Alexander III.5.1–3 Spengel), and in another ancient novel we find a conversation reminiscent of Longus 2.7: in the novel of Chariton the king of Persia tells his faithful eunuch of his love for Callirhoe in a roundabout way − τίς γάρ ἐστιν Ἔρως πρότερον ἤκουον ἐν μύθοις[50] τε καὶ ποιήμασιν, ὅτι κρατεῖ πάντων τῶν θεῶν καὶ αὐτοῦ τοῦ Διός (6.3.2). When the truth has finally emerged the king asks the eunuch to find a φάρμακον for his love, but the eunuch knows that φάρμακον ἕτερον Ἔρωτος οὐδέν ἐστι πλὴν αὐτὸς ὁ ἐρώμενος (6.3.7, cf. Longus 2.7.7). The doubts that these passages may raise about the implications of Philetas' language are reinforced by an examination of the standard language of praise in the rhetorical literature of the Empire. Menander tells prospective orators how to praise Γάμος:[51]

τὰ δὲ μετὰ τὰ προοίμια ἔστω περὶ τοῦ θεοῦ τοῦ γάμου λόγος ὥσπερ θετικὸς καθόλου τὴν ἐξέτασιν περιέχων ὅτι καλὸν ὁ γάμος, ἄρξηι δὲ ἄνωθεν, ὅτι μετὰ τὴν λύσιν τοῦ χάους εὐθὺς ὑπὸ τῆς φύσεως ἐδημιουργήθη ὁ γάμος, εἰ δὲ βούλει, ὡς Ἐμπεδοκλῆς φησι, καὶ ⟨ὁ⟩ ἔρως. γενόμενος δὲ ὁ θεὸς οὗτος συνάπτει μὲν οὐρανὸν τῆι γῆι, συνάπτει δὲ Κρόνον τῆι Ῥέαι, συνεργοῦντος αὐτῶι πρὸς ταῦτα τοῦ ἔρωτος · εἶτα ἐφεξῆς ἐρεῖς ὅτι ἡ τῶν ὅλων διακόσμησις διὰ τὸν γάμον γέγονεν, ἀέρος, ἀστέρων, θαλάσσης· τοῦ γὰρ θεοῦ τούτου τὴν στάσιν παύσαντος καὶ συνάψαντος ὁμονοίαι καὶ τελετῆι γαμηλίωι τὸν οὐρανὸν πρὸς τὴν γῆν, ἅπαντα διεκρίθη καὶ στάσιν οἰκείαν ἔλαβεν. ὑποβαίνων δὲ πάλιν ἐρεῖς ἐξ ἀκολουθίας ὅτι καὶ αὐτὸς τῆι βασιλείαι τῶν ὅλων τὸν Δία δημιουργήσας ἐπέστησε, καὶ οὐκ ἄχρι τῶν θεῶν ἔστη μόνον, ἀλλὰ καὶ τοὺς ἡμιθέους αὐτὸς παρήγαγεν πείσας θεοὺς συνελθεῖν τοὺς μὲν γυναιξί, τοὺς δὲ νύμφαις. μετὰ ταῦτα πάλιν ἐρεῖς ὅτι αὐτὸς τὸν ἄνθρωπον ὁμοίως φῦσαι παρεσκεύασε καὶ σχεδὸν ἀθάνατον ἐφιλοτέχνησε, συμπαραπέμπων ἀεὶ τὰς διαδοχὰς τοῦ γένους τῶι μήκει τοῦ χρόνου, καὶ ὅτι βελτίων Προμηθέως ἡμῖν· ὁ μὲν γὰρ τὸ πῦρ μόνον κλέψας ἔδωκεν, ὁ δὲ γάμος ἀθανασίαν ἡμῖν πορίζεται. ἐμπλεονάσεις δὲ τούτωι τῶι μέρει δεικνὺς ὅτι δι᾽ αὐτὸν θάλαττα πλεῖται, δι᾽ αὐτὸν γεωργεῖται γῆ, ὅτι φιλοσοφία καὶ γνῶσις τῶν οὐρανίων δι᾽ ἐκεῖνόν ἐστι καὶ νόμοι καὶ πολιτεῖαι καὶ πάντα ἁπλῶς τὰ ἀνθρώπινα· εἶτα οὐδὲ μέχρι τούτων στήσηι, ἀλλ᾽ ὅτι καὶ μέχρι πηγῶν καὶ ποταμῶν διικνεῖται ὁ θεὸς καὶ νηκτῶν καὶ χερσαίων καὶ ἀερίων.

(Men. Rhet. 401 Sp.–RW)

Of particular interest in this regard are the prose 'hymns' of Aristeides (*Or.* 37–46 K). In these attempts to rival the language and function of poetry[52] there are many examples of extravagant praise which remind us of Philetas' description of the powers of Eros. As Boulanger remarks, 'celui qu'il célèbre est toujours le plus puissant et le plus bienfaisant de tous'.[53] Worthy of quotation here is a passage from the peroration to the *Hymn to Dionysus*:

ὁ δὲ θαυμαστὸς ἀνθρώπων τύραννος Ἔρως ἐκ Διονύσου πηγῶν ἀρυσάμενος γῆν ἅπασαν ἐπέρχεται προηγητῆι τῶι Διονύσωι χρώμενος, οὐδ᾽ αὐτῶι θᾶκοι τούτου χωρὶς οὐδ᾽ ἔργα οὐδ᾽ εὐναί. νυκτὸς τοίνυν καὶ ἡμέρας πέρατα ἐπισκοπεῖ, τὴν μὲν αὐτὸς δαιδοῦχός τε καὶ ἡγεμὼν τῆς ὄψεως γιγνόμενος, τὴν δὲ ἑτέροις παριείς· ἀργῶν δ᾽ ὅμως οὐδ᾽ οὕτως, ἀεὶ δ᾽ ἐν φορᾶι καὶ κινήσει τὸν αἰῶνα διεξέρχεται. πρεσβύτατος δὲ ὢν θεῶν αὐτὸς καὶ νεώτατός ἐστιν, τῆς δ᾽ ἀεὶ παρούσης ὥρας καὶ μοίρας φίλος.

(Aristeides, *Or.* 41.12–13 K)

This passage shares with Longus both certain ideas about Eros (his connection with Dionysus, his paradoxical age) and a debt to Plato's *Symposium*,[54] and it illustrates clearly the well-trodden path which the Longan Philetas follows. It must be stressed again that the fact that Philetas' language

35

in 2.4–7 is of such common currency does not necessarily rule out a real 'religious meaning' for it, nor even make this inherently improbable. We are, however, entitled to wonder whether all of Longus' readers would have seen in Philetas' speech the same religious force that some modern critics have found. The 'Orphic' ideas of 2.5.2 are soon forgotten (cf. 2.7.1 θεός ... νέος ... καὶ νεότητι χαίρει), and it is once again the little boy who leaps away καθάπερ ἀηδόνος νεοττός when he has finished with Philetas (2.6.1)[55] and who puts away his bow and quiver when he has finished his sport with Daphnis and Chloe (4.34.1). Longus' Eros is a mixture of traits and hints derived from a variety of traditions and no attempt to put an interpretative straitjacket on him will succeed.[56]

After their marriage Daphnis and Chloe establish an altar to Ἔρως ποιμήν (4.39.2). In his address to Philetas Eros himself declares νῦν δὲ Δάφνιν ποιμαίνω καὶ Χλόην (2.5.4)[57] and in the third book Daphnis and Chloe are the first to be out in the new spring οἷα μείζονι δουλεύοντες ποιμένι (3.12.1).[58] This notion is both suitably bucolic and does indeed suggest the caring deity of the mystery religions. It was, however, not entirely new to literature. Already in Pindar the Erotes are described in the following metaphorical terms, οἷοι καὶ Διὸς Αἰγίνας τε λέκτρον|ποιμένες ἀμφεπόλησαν|Κυπρίας δώρων (Nem. 8.6–7), and a rather banal epigram of late Hellenistic date describes a painting in which Eros guards the flocks while the shepherd sleeps (Myrinus, AP 7.703 = GP 2568). A similar idea may lie behind Tibullus' amusing sketch,

> ipse quoque inter agros interque armenta Cupido
> natus et indomitas dicitur inter equas.
> illic indocto primum se exercuit arcu:
> ei mihi, quam doctas nunc habet ille manus.

(2.1.67–70)

In the Critias Plato describes how the gods cared for early man as a shepherd cares for his flock (109b–c), and Maximus of Tyre compares the love of Socrates for his ἐρώμενοι to that of a shepherd for his sheep (19.2 H). We must again conclude that, while Longus certainly 'plays' with words of religious and mystical content, he never moves beyond general notions that would be familiar to any educated reader.[59] What we admire is the novelty of the whole, rather than that of any of the parts.

Of the other gods in the novel, Pan and the Nymphs appear in a very traditional guise. There is no sign of the cosmic role which was assigned to Pan in certain later cults of 'Orphic' type,[60] and the joint forces of Pan, Eros and the Nymphs inevitably remind us of the 'boy gets girl with divine assistance' plot of Menander's *Dyscolus* (although no direct influence from this comedy need be postulated). These divinities all have traditional links with Dionysus,[61] the god whose power can be felt throughout the novel and not merely in the fourth book where it is most obvious. Dionysus was an important god in the Lesbos of the imperial period:[62] there was a very ancient shrine of the god at Brisa, and Zeus, Hera and Dionysus shared another sanctuary which has been made famous by the poetry of Sappho (fr. 17 LP–V) and Alcaeus (fr. 129 LP–V). In *D&C* Dionysus is omnipresent. The description of the vintage at the opening of the second book suggests this god to us and, more directly, the female workers compare Daphnis' beauty to that of Dionysus and the male workers act towards Chloe like satyrs towards a bacchant (2.2.1–2, cf. 1.23.3). In the third book Daphnis is lucky enough to find Chloe's family celebrating the winter *Dionysia* (3.9–10) – we are obviously to understand that the children, like Dionysus, will have their chance again when spring comes (but cf. also pp. 10–11 above on this passage). Eros and Dionysus are further linked by the parallel descriptions in Books 2 and 4 of Philetas' garden, in which Eros plays, and Lamon's garden with its shrine of Dionysus. A particularly sophisticated link between Pan and Dionysus is forged by the device of using material from the *Homeric Hymn to Dionysus* in the account of Pan's attack on the Methymnaeans to rescue Chloe,[63] just as the same poem was echoed at the start of Daphnis' corresponding adventure in the first book (cf. below p. 61). Like Pan, Dionysus was closely connected with music and poetry, both in real cult (as witness the great dramatic festivals in Athens), and in literature,[64] and his dominant influence requires no special justification in a novel which is largely concerned with love and music.

If the ceaseless seasonal round naturally suggests Dionysus to us and this god has a temple in the middle of the garden of Lamon,[65] we may well wonder at the significance of the name of the owner of the estate and Daphnis' real father, Dionysophanes. This grand, aristocratic name is known to have belonged to real people and is of a familiar type.[66] Of particular interest is the fact that this was the name of the father of Praxiphanes, the famous Peripatetic scholar and critic of the third century B.C.;[67] Praxiphanes is regularly designated a Mytilenean in our sources and this gives us a connection for the name Dionysophanes with Lesbos, or at least with the eastern Aegean. This name is therefore a realistic as well as a 'mystical' element in the novel. There is certainly nothing 'mystical' about the names of the other characters who appear for the first time in the fourth book (cf. below pp. 67–9), and there is nothing in Dionysophanes' behaviour on the estate to suggest that he is in any sense a personification of divine forces, let alone a god (*the* god) himself.[68] The religious element of his name merely teases us and is one of many which go to make up a complex literary character. We smile when we recognise in the name Dionysophanes a 'religious' strand which had appeared earlier also in the novel, but we shall be very disappointed if we think that this strand can unravel or even impose a pattern on a large part of it.[69]

(iv) *The prologue*

D&C is presented as the story lying behind a painting of a series of disparate but related scenes which the author claims to have seen in a grove of the Nymphs while he was hunting on Lesbos. The novel therefore differs from, although it is obviously related to, the many descriptions of works of art in literature which illustrate or foreshadow themes of the works in which they appear but which provide only one element of a complex whole; the earliest and best-known example is the description of the Shield of Achilles in *Iliad* 18.[70] Of particular interest is the opening of Achilles Tatius' novel in which the author and narrator meet each other while they are both looking at a painting which illustrates the power of Eros.[71] In the stratagem of both Longus and Achilles Perry sees a device for avoiding having to tell a lengthy and serious fictitious narrative in the first person, which would breach the literary propriety which charged the author with responsibility for the truth of what he asserted: '[Longus] has the sensibility of an educated man trained in the academic tradition, for whom a narrative in prose, unlike a drama, is necessarily a history in theory. It must be formally vouched for as true in substance, either by the author himself in his own person . . . or by some other authority, man or document, in this case a picture, to which the author refers.'[72] Perry's investigation of this ancient narrative mode is very enlightening, and it is hardly to be doubted that behind the procedure of Longus and Achilles does lie academic theorising of this kind, particularly in view of Longus' use in the prologue of the historiographical tradition (cf. below pp. 48–50). Nevertheless, the explanation for Longus' choice of this form of narrative is not to be sought solely in academic doctrine about literary propriety, but rather in the very themes and ideas of the novel itself, and it is this which I wish to explore in the present section. As for Achilles' decision to use a first-person narrative told to 'the author', we should bear in mind not only literary theory but also the fact that this device calls the reader's attention to the interest and amusement of the story which is to follow, i.e. the interest taken by 'the author' in the narrator's story invites the reader's interest in it. This is a classic device of the literary tale, and is well illustrated, for example, throughout the *Metamorphoses* of Apuleius in which the narrator often becomes a listener. Achilles was perhaps also influenced by the humorous (not to say scandalous) nature of the tale which he has to tell. Similarly, critics might be slower to castigate Achilles for failing at the end of his novel to recur to the initial conversation if they were to reflect that similar *neglegentia* is found in Plato (cf. *Symposium*, *Protagoras*), who was very likely Achilles' model for this technique, and is the regular practice of Greek epic poets.[73]

Whatever the relationship between Longus' narrative style and ancient 'narrative' painting may be (cf. above pp. 4–6), it is clear that in the prologue Longus reflects the practice of those ancient writers and orators who attempted to make their audience see important incidents 'with the mind's eye', to make them visualise events. Xenophon of Ephesus, for example, calls attention to particular descriptions by the introductory formula ἦν ... τὸ θέαμα ἐλεεινόν (cf. 1.14.2, 2.6.3), and in one of Himerius' declamations the speaker imagines the whole of his unhappy story, which in fact includes the exposure and recovery of children as in *D&C*, as a series of painted scenes (4.24–6 Colonna). This concern for narrative ἐνάργεια is well described in Plutarch's analysis of the power of Thucydides' writing[74] (he is discussing the similarities between poetry and painting): τέλος δ' ἀμφοτέροις ἓν ὑπόκειται, καὶ τῶν ἱστορικῶν κράτιστος ὁ τὴν διήγησιν ὥσπερ γραφὴν πάθεσι καὶ προσώποις εἰδωλοποιήσας. ὁ δ' οὖν Θουκυδίδης ἀεὶ τῶι λόγωι πρὸς ταύτην ἁμιλλᾶται τὴν ἐνάργειαν, οἷον θεατὴν ποιῆσαι τὸν ἀκροατὴν καὶ τὰ γιγνόμενα περὶ τοὺς ὁρῶντας ἐκπληκτικὰ καὶ ταρακτικὰ πάθη τοῖς ἀναγιγνώσκουσιν ἐνεργάσασθαι λιχνευόμενος (*Mor.* 347a). The list of examples of this concern for visual power in fictional writing could be greatly multiplied, but I mention only two interesting cases. At 5.8.2 Chariton compares the emotional scene in the court-room at Babylon to a scene in a play, τίς ἂν φράσαι κατ' ἀξίαν ἐκεῖνο τὸ σχῆμα τοῦ δικαστηρίου; ποῖος ποιητὴς ἐπὶ σκηνῆς παράδοξον μῦθον οὕτως εἰσήγαγεν; ἔδοξας ἂν ἐν θεάτρωι παρεῖναι μυρίων παθῶν πλήρει · πάντα ἦν ὁμοῦ, δάκρυα, χαρά, θάμβος, ἔλεος, ἀπιστία, εὐχαί. Here Chariton makes us see the events 'from the gallery' and exploits the natural similarity between a law-court and a theatre. Secondly, at the opening of Heliodorus' novel a 'tableau vivant' of destruction on a beach is presented to us as a scene observed by others, and this directs our attention to the visual side of the description, cf. 1.1.6 καὶ μυρίον εἶδος ὁ δαίμων ἐπὶ μικροῦ τοῦ χωρίου διεσκεύαστο, φόνους καὶ πότους, σπονδὰς καὶ σφαγὰς ἐπισυνάψας, καὶ τοιοῦτον θέατρον λῃσταῖς Αἰγυπτίοις ἐπιδείξας. It is hard to believe that Heliodorus was not influenced in this passage by the use of the descriptions of paintings as an introductory device in works such as that of Achilles Tatius.[75]

The fact that the whole of *D&C* is in effect a 'work of art' lends particular force to its role as an ἀνάθημα, or 'dedication', to Love, the Nymphs and Pan (*Proem* 3), since ἀναθήματα were normally solid objects placed by devotees in the gods' shrines (cf. 1.4.3). In return for this offering Longus asks for a specific benefit, ἡμῖν δ' ὁ θεὸς παράσχοι σωφρονοῦσι τὰ τῶν ἄλλων γράφειν. In writing about a god (in this case Eros) one risks incurring the anger of that god, which in this case would be manifested as a destructive love affair, i.e. a lack of σωφροσύνη.[76] We may compare Catullus' prayer at the end of his narrative of the miserable fate of Attis:

> dea, magna dea, Cybebe, dea domina Dindymi
> procul a mea tuos sit furor omnis, era, domo:
> alios age incitatos, alios age rabidos. (63.91-3)

A further parallel of some interest is an epigram by Agathias in which he dedicates his Δαφνιακά to Aphrodite (cf. above p. 23):

> Δαφνιακῶν βίβλων Ἀγαθηϊὰς ἐννεὰς εἰμι·
> ἀλλά μ' ὁ τεκτήνας ἄνθετο σοί, Παφίη.
> οὐ γὰρ Πιερίδεσσι τόσον μέλω, ὅσσον Ἔρωτι,
> ὄργια τοσσατίων ἀμφιέπουσα πόθων.
> αἰτεῖ δ' ἀντὶ πόνων, ἵνα οἱ διὰ σεῖο παρείη
> ἤ τινα μὴ φιλέειν ἤ ταχὺ πειθομένην.

(*AP* 6.80 = 4 Viansino)

This poem asks Aphrodite for an easy love-life in return for the poet's πόνοι (cf. *D&C Proem* 3 ἐξεπονησάμην); only a

greater knowledge of the Δαφνιακά than we possess would
enable us to discover whether Agathias has here been influenced by Longus' prologue or whether they are independent
reflections of a common idea. What we ought, however, to
note about Longus' prayer is that, unlike Catullus' wish at
the end of Poem 63 and unlike the desire of the chorus at
E. *Hipp.* 528–9, μή μοι ποτὲ σὺν κακῶι φανείης [sc. Ἔρως]|
μηδ᾽ ἄρρυθμος ἔλθοις, it is not prompted by evidence of the
destructive power of Eros, and neither Longus nor his readers
are ever likely to be 'afflicted' with the experiences of
Daphnis and Chloe. Longus here puts an ironic distance
between himself and his narrative, a distance which we come
to recognise as typical of him: it may be true that οὐδεὶς
Ἔρωτα ἔφυγεν ἢ φεύξεται,[77] but on the evidence of this
novel no one would wish to.

The idea of the novel as a painting is exploited by Longus
in two main ways. First, a painting occupies a definite space
(even it if extends over several walls) and is not open-ended.
So also Longus' Lesbos is essentially a closed world. It is
not necessary to follow certain critics in regarding Lamon's
luxurious garden (4.2–3) as a microcosmic representation
of this world in order to appreciate the advantages that
Longus has gained by localising his narrative within a small
geographical area: he has symbolised the enclosed world of
his protagonists by setting them within the defined space of
a painting. The adventures of Daphnis and Chloe are similarly
set within a clear frame. Whether we wish to call this story
a description of the change from innocence to experience[78]
or simply a titillating tale about the loss of virginity, there is
a real sense in which the wedding-night is the conclusion to
which the whole work leads and, although we are told by
the author that Daphnis and Chloe are going to allow their
children to enjoy the same pleasures that they did, it is
hard to imagine how the story could have continued after
their night of love. After their marriage the happy couple
set up εἰκόνες in the cave of the Nymphs (4.39.2) and,
although Longus does not mention a cave in the ἄλσος of
the prooemium, it is hardly fanciful to equate the εἰκόνες

with the painting of which the whole novel is a description. By this act the children acknowledge that what has happened to them is final. You only grow up once.

In setting his novel to vie with the visual appeal of a painting, Longus employs a mild form of the sort of self-advertisement used by Aelian in introducing his description of the Vale of Tempe, τὰ καλούμενα Τέμπη τὰ Θετταλικὰ διαγράψωμεν τῶι λόγωι καὶ διαπλάσωμεν· ὡμολόγηται γὰρ καὶ ὁ λόγος, ἐὰν ἔχηι δύναμιν φραστικήν, μηδὲν ἀσθενέστερον ὅσα βούλεται δεικνύναι τῶν ἀνδρῶν τῶν κατὰ χειρουργίαν δεινῶν (VH 3.1), or by Lucian in the introduction to a description of a marvellously ornate room, τὸ χαλεπὸν δὲ τοῦ τολμήματος ὁρᾶτε, ἄνευ χρωμάτων καὶ σχημάτων καὶ τόπου συστήσασθαι τοσαύτας εἰκόνας· ψιλὴ γάρ τις ἡ γραφὴ τῶν λόγων (de domo 21), or by the speaker in the following passage of Himerius, φέρε δὴ γράψω τῶι λόγωι τὸν πίνακα· ἔχει γὰρ οἶμαι πρὸς μίμησιν οἰκεῖα καὶ λόγος φάρμακα ... οὐκοῦν δότε μοι τὴν Ζεύξιδος τέχνην, τὰ Παρρασίου σοφίσματα (12.2–5 Colonna). I shall return presently to the idea of μίμησις which is introduced in this last passage, but first we may note how the identification of novel and painting is both reinforced by the language which Longus uses and exploited linguistically by him. The fact that γράφειν means both 'to write' and 'to paint' allowed much room for the sort of play which we find at Lucian, Imag. 8 where Homer's description of colour makes him the best γραφεύς among painters.[79] For Longus this ambiguity means that in describing the γραφή on Lesbos as τερπνοτέρα καὶ τέχνην ἔχουσα περιττὴν καὶ τύχην ἐρωτικήν he is also in these words advertising the pleasures and substance of his novel. A more subtle web binds the pregnant phrase εἰκόνος γραφήν, ἱστορίαν ἔρωτος.[80] The first half means, with reference to the painting, 'a painted description' but perhaps also hints at the novel as a 'description of a painting'. In later Greek ἱστορία appears with the sense 'story told in a work of art' (Ach. Tat. 5.4.1, Nicolaus III p. 492.16 Sp.) and then in the Byzantine period ἱστορεῖν can mean 'to paint' and ἱστορία 'a painting'.[81] It seems that Longus here foreshadows this development in the word's application and he has used it to create the same relationship between writing and painting in both halves of the phrase: ἱστορία ἔρωτος is both 'an account of love' and a 'picture of love'. The equivalence of γραφή and ἱστορία also throws light on the parallelism of εἰκόνος and ἔρωτος. Just as the painting represents ἔρως, so too does the literary εἰκών: as Homer painted an εἰκών ... χρηστοῦ βίου καὶ ἀρετῆς ἀκριβοῦς (Max. Tyr. 26.6b H), so Longus creates an εἰκών ἔρωτος. The idea of literature as an εἰκών was a very old one – Isocrates described the *Antidosis* as a λόγος ὥσπερ εἰκὼν τῆς ἐμῆς διανοίας καὶ τῶν ἄλλων τῶν ἐμοὶ βεβιωμένων, which will be πολὺ κάλλιον τῶν χαλκῶν ἀναθημάτων (*Antid.* 7)[82] – and it is interesting to note that Apuleius has used a related device: as Charite flees from the robbers' cave she promises Lucius that she will put up in her house a painting of their escape and *uisetur et in fabulis audietur doctorumque stilis rudis perpetuabitur historia 'asino uectore uirgo regia fugiens captiuitatem'* (*Met.* 6.29). So also in Longus the tourists come to Lesbos[83] to admire the painted εἰκών, πολλοὶ καὶ τῶν ξένων κατὰ φήμην ἤιεσαν, τῶν μὲν Νυμφῶν ἱκέται, τῆς δὲ εἰκόνος θεαταί, just as we will both read and 'see' the literary εἰκών. The notion of the novel as an εἰκών also reminds us of the doctrine of μίμησις and this is part of the second major function of Longus' presentation of his work as a painting.

The link between poetry and painting was commented upon at least as early as the famous dictum of Simonides that painting was silent poetry and poetry painting that talked.[84] How banal this thought had become is illustrated by the following verses from a poem of the fourth century A.D. in honour of a former professor at the university at Berytus:

> ἐπαινετέον δὲ τῶν μαθητῶν τὸν χορὸν
> εὐγνωμοσύνης τῆς ἀμφὶ τὸν διδάσκαλον.
> ἄλλως γὰρ αὐτὸν οὐκ ἔχοντες εἰσορᾶν
> ἔστησαν ἐν γραφαῖσιν εἰκόνων δύο,
> ὧν τὴν μὲν ἠργάσαντο παῖδες ζωγράφων,
> ἡ δ' ἥν ἐν ἑκάστωι κατὰ φύσιν γεγραμμένη
> ἐν τῆι διανοίαι. νῦν δ' ἐγὼ ταύτην τρίτην

ἔμπνουν ἀναθήσω καὶ λαλοῦσαν εἰκόνα,
οὗτοι διατήξας κηρόν, ἀλλ᾽ εἰπὼν ἔπη.

(*GDRK* XXX. 16–24 Heitsch)

Banal it may have been, but the link between the mimetic arts of poetry and painting is fully explored and exploited by Longus. In Book 10 of the *Republic* Plato uses painting as his main analogy for literature as μίμησις, and echoes of this are found throughout subsequent rhetorical and critical literature.[85] I have already noted the place of μίμησις in the education of the children (cf. above pp. 19–20) – imitation teaches them everything except how to make love, an activity which requires the τέχνη ἐρωτική, and it is clear that the relationship between φύσις and τέχνη is a dominant theme of the novel, as indeed of nearly all bucolic and pastoral literature in which 'artists' seek to portray a 'natural' world.[86] The ancients often thought of the arts as imitative of nature[87] and it is noteworthy that 'Longinus' was able to combine Aristotelian and rhetorical μίμησις into a literary theory (he is discussing hyperbaton), παρὰ τοῖς ἀρίστοις συγγραφεῦσι διὰ τῶν ὑπερβάτων ἡ μίμησις ἐπὶ τὰ τῆς φύσεως ἔργα φέρεται. τότε γὰρ ἡ τέχνη τέλεως ἡνίκ᾽ ἂν φύσις εἶναι δοκῇ, ἡ δ᾽ αὖ φύσις ἐπιτυχὴς ὅταν λανθάνουσαν περιέχηι τὴν τέχνην (*de subl.* 22.1).[88] In the artificial world of sophistic rhetoric such notions would have a peculiar importance, even if they now lacked the intellectual and critical context in which the author of *On the sublime* had set them. Longus constantly reminds us of the interplay of φύσις and τέχνη, cf., e.g., 4.2.5 of the trees in Lamon's garden, ἐδόκει μέντοι καὶ ἡ τούτων φύσις εἶναι τέχνης; in this world even nature can practice μίμησις (cf. 4.2.3 and p. 73 below). This tension between φύσις and τέχνη is also reflected in the very artificial form in which the 'natural' education of the children is described: the highly wrought verbal and stylistic sophistication of the novel is, as in Theocritus, set in pointed opposition to the simple, 'natural' subject-matter. Longus signals this tension by presenting his novel as an elaborate work of art, a novel containing both τέχνην περιττήν and τύχην ἐρωτικήν.[89] As a description of a painting the novel is at two (or, in Platonic terms, three) removes from reality (or φύσις) in being the result of two separate acts of μίμησις, and so Longus' prologue device is seen to be directly related to the major themes of this playful work.

The Greek philosophical tradition had long used allegorical paintings and stories as didactic tools and this has not unnaturally raised the question of the status of *D&C* as an allegory. It is the Stoics who are most associated with the allegorical interpretation of both painting and literature, but the principles of this method were widely familiar in the second century A.D.[90] Chalk certainly goes too far in concluding from the fact that everything on the painting was ἐρωτικά (*Proem* 2) that 'allegorization is in principle justified'.[91] This statement need mean no more than that everything in the novel is part, as it obviously is, of the ἱστορία ἔρωτος. Moreover, as *D&C* is overtly concerned with *eros*, the movement of the seasons and things Dionysiac in general, we may wonder whether the term 'allegory' is appropriate here, in either its ancient or modern sense. For the ancients ἀλληγορία was simply 'saying one thing and meaning another',[92] and it is my impression that this is not something which Longus often does. The 'mystical' element in the novel is something to which Longus openly calls our attention in unambiguous language. Further support for the view that Longus wants us to see his painting/novel as an allegory has been found in the fact that he needed an ἐξηγητής to explain the painting to him, but this word need mean no more than 'museum guide'[93] and the necessity for such a guide is, in the context of the fiction which Longus sets up, an obvious one; the narrator has added the τέχνη (cf. ἐξεπονησάμην)[94] to a local μῦθος or ἱστορία, and the need for someone else to tell him the story stresses its mythical or legendary status. The story of the two children had established itself as a μῦθος on Lesbos long before the narrator came upon it. To what, if any, extent Longus did in fact use material from local historians and compilers of Λεσβιακά[95] we cannot tell, but it is clear that this is the sort of flavour which he sought to give to his narrative (cf. above p. 17 on the name Nape). An 'allegorical' interpretation is certainly not demanded by the prologue or even suggested by the scenes on the painting which the narrator lists,[96] but *more suo* Longus has hinted at a second and deeper level of meaning which he challenges us to pursue; the quarry, however, remains pleasantly elusive.

The element of τὸ τερπνόν in the novel/painting (γραφὴ τερπνοτέρα, κτῆμα τερπνόν) associates the work with the poetic tradition and, in particular, with the 'poetic licence' which is a standard theme in ancient criticism.[97] In the *Ars Poetica* Horace associates *ficta* with *uoluptas* (vv. 333–46), and the following passage of Lucian may serve as a representative of the standard view, οὐ γὰρ ἀληθείας μέλει [sc. τοῖς ποιηταῖς] . . . ἀλλὰ τοῦ κηλεῖν τοὺς ἀκούοντας, καὶ διὰ τοῦτο μέτροις τε κατάιδουσι καὶ μύθοις κατηχοῦσι καὶ ὅλως ἅπαντα ὑπὲρ τοῦ τερπνοῦ μηχανῶνται (*Zeus trag.* 39, cf. *Philopseud.* 4, Isocr. *ad Nicoclem* 48, Dio Chrys. 11.42 etc.); in his guide to the way in which young men should study poetry Plutarch also stresses at length the falsehoods with which poetry is filled (*Mor.* 16a–f). Longus thus hints clearly at the entirely fictitious nature of the narrative which is to follow[98] and this is particularly important in view of the fun which he is to have a few lines later in the prologue with the historiographical tradition (cf. below p. 48–50). Achilles Tatius performs the same task with characteristic wit when Cleitophon replies to the narrator's request for information with the remark σμῆνος ἀνεγείρεις . . . λόγων· τὰ γὰρ ἐμὰ μύθοις ἔοικε (1.2.2), and it is equally amusing in *D&C* when Dionysophanes forbids Lamon ὅμοια πλάττειν μύθοις (with reference to the story of Daphnis' exposure) in an attempt to hold on to his foster-son (4.20.1). Achilles' antithesis between μῦθος and λόγος, which, like σμῆνος ἀνεγείρεις λόγων, he owes to Plato,[99] appears in *D&C* at 2.7.1 just after Philetas has told Daphnis and Chloe of his encounter with Eros, πάνυ ἐτέρφθησαν ὥσπερ μῦθον οὐ λόγον ἀκούοντες: here again τὸ τερπνόν is associated with falsehood. For the rhetoricians a μῦθος was a λόγος ψευδὴς εἰκονίζων ἀλήθειαν,[100] but Longus is not even much

47

concerned consistently to preserve the second part of this definition. In his prologue Apuleius also stresses the pleasure to be derived from his work, *auresque tuas beniuolas lepido susurro permulceam . . . lector intende: laetaberis (Met.* 1.1), and in dismissing comedies and romances as falsehoods designed only for the pleasure of the hearer Macrobius (*Somn.Scip.* 1.2.7–8) perhaps echoes Apuleius' words.[101] Apuleius, of course, makes it abundantly clear in the opening section of his novel that his work will be entirely fictitious (cf. 1.2–3, 5, 20). With Longus, Achilles and Apuleius may be contrasted Chariton, who begins his narrative by announcing its strict historicity (πάθος ἐρωτικὸν ἐν Συρρακούσαις γενόμενον διηγήσομαι 1.1.1).

This is the background against which we must interpret Longus' description of his work and its utility: τέτταρας βίβλους ἐξεπονησάμην, ἀνάθημα μὲν Ἔρωτι καὶ Νύμφαις καὶ Πανί, κτῆμα δὲ τερπνὸν πᾶσιν ἀνθρώποις, ὃ καὶ νοσοῦντα ἰάσεται καὶ λυπούμενον παραμυθήσεται, τὸν ἐρασθέντα ἀναμνήσει, τὸν οὐκ ἐρασθέντα προπαιδεύσει (*Proem* 3). The form of this sentence may remind us of Isocrates' prefatory remarks to his *Epistle to Demonicus*, ἀπέσταλκά σοι τόνδε τὸν λόγον δῶρον, τεκμήριον μὲν τῆς πρὸς ὑμᾶς εὐνοίας, σημεῖον δὲ τῆς πρὸς Ἱππόνικον συνηθείας, but it was suggested long ago[102] that Longus is here thinking of Thucydides' claim in 1.22 to write a κτῆμα ἐς αἰεί, and this seems certainly correct when we add the historian's description of his work in the same chapter, ἐς μὲν ἀκρόασιν ἴσως τὸ μὴ μυθῶδες αὐτῶν ἀτερπέστερον φανεῖται· ὅσοι δὲ βουλήσονται τῶν τε γενομένων τὸ σαφὲς σκοπεῖν καὶ τῶν μελλόντων ποτὲ αὖθις . . . τοιούτων καὶ παραπλησίων ἔσεσθαι, ὠφέλιμα κρίνειν κτλ. The Thucydidean distinction between, on the one hand, τὸ μυθῶδες and τὸ ἡδύ and, on the other, τὸ μὴ μυθῶδες and τὸ ὠφέλιμον recurs quite clearly in the opening section of Isocrates' *Panathenaicus*[103] and was a focal point for historiographical dispute throughout the Hellenistic period.[104] Polybius, for example, explicitly sets out to provide his readers with τὸ χρήσιμον καὶ τὸ τερπνόν (1.4.11, cf. 3.31.2), as indeed does Longus; in introducing his account of the courage of women, Plutarch similarly echoes Thucydides' words, while not forsaking entirely a claim to give delight:

τὰ ὑπόλοιπα τῶν λεγομένων εἰς τὸ μίαν εἶναι καὶ τὴν αὐτὴν ἀνδρός τε καὶ γυναικὸς ἀρετὴν προσανέγραψά σοι, τὸ ἱστορικὸν ἀποδεικτικὸν ἔχοντα καὶ πρὸς ἡδονὴν μὲν ἀκοῆς οὐ συντεταγμένον, εἰ δὲ τῶι πείθοντι καὶ τὸ τέρπον ἔνεστι φύσει τοῦ παραδείγματος, οὐ φεύγει χάριν ἀποδείξεως συνεργὸν ὁ λόγος οὐδ᾽ αἰσχύνεται ᾽ταῖς Μούσαις τὰς Χάριτας συγκαταμιγνὺς καλλίστην συζυγίαν᾽ ὡς Εὐριπίδης φησίν (HF 673-4), ἐκ τοῦ φιλοκάλου μάλιστα τῆς ψυχῆς ἀναδούμενος τὴν πίστιν.

(Plutarch, Mor. 242f-3a)

Needless to say, the distinctions between poetry and history were in reality not nearly so clear as the theoreticians made them,[105] and the very strict divorce between the two which Lucian demands in On the writing of history (especially paragraphs 8-10) is an entirely unrealistic proposal.

By stressing the element of τὸ τερπνόν within an allusion to Thucydides, Longus aligns his work with that of Herodotus, whom ancient scholars saw as the object of Thucydides' attack in 1.22 (cf. Σ Thucyd. 1.22.4) and whom Lucian describes in terms normally reserved for poets, ἄιδων τὰς ἱστορίας καὶ κηλῶν τοὺς παρόντας (Lucian, Hdt. 1). I discuss elsewhere Longus' adoption of an 'Herodotean' style (cf. below pp. 96-7) and so I shall confine my remarks here to the debt which Longus owes to Thucydides. I begin with the scholia to the relevant part of Thucyd. 1.22:

κτῆμα   κτῆμα τὴν ἀλήθειαν, ἀγώνισμα τὸν γλυκὺν λόγον. αἰνίττεται δὲ τὰ μυθικὰ Ἡροδότου. //διὰ τοῦτο Διονύσιος περὶ Δημοσθένους (Dion. Hal. Dem. 10, I p. 149 U-R) φησί·οὐκ ἀνάθημα ποιῶν τὸν λόγον ὡς ὁ συγγραφεύς.
ἀγώνισμα   θέαμα, παιδιά, ποιητικὸν ἀγώνισμα κωμωιδοποιῶν ἢ τραγωιδοποιῶν.

The points of contact between these scholia and the proem of D&C are at least suggestive: the gloss θέαμα for ἀγώνισμα may serve as a reminder that θέαμα κάλλιστον in Longus refers as much to the novel as to the painting which it purports to describe. A θέαμα is a 'marvel which gives pleasure' (LSJ

49

s.v.) and, although its reference is normally visual (cf., e.g., Theocr. 1.56), in Longus it forms a neat ring with the closing words of the novel, ποιμένων παίγνια, part of whose function is to point the reader to a level at which the work may be interpreted, just as Gorgias concludes the *Helen* with the words ἐβουλήθην γράψαι τὸν λόγον Ἑλένης μὲν ἐγκώμιον, ἐμὸν δὲ παίγνιον.[106] Secondly, the scholia to Thucydides cite part of the following sentence from Dionysius of Halicarnassus: ὁ δὲ ῥήτωρ τοῦ τε [Sylburg: δὲ codd.] ἀρκοῦντος στοχάζεται καὶ τοὺς καιροὺς συμμετρεῖται οὐκ εἰς ἀνάθημα καὶ κτῆμα κα⟨τασκευάζων⟩ [*suppl.* Sylburg] τὴν λέξιν μόνον ὥσπερ ὁ συγγραφεύς, ἀλλὰ καὶ εἰς χρῆσιν. In view of the other links between these scholia and the proem of *D&C*, it does not seem fanciful to suggest that Longus has this passage of Dionysius (or a quotation of it) in mind when describing his work as an ἀνάθημα μὲν Ἔρωτι καὶ Νύμφαις καὶ Πανί, κτῆμα δὲ τερπνὸν πᾶσιν ἀνθρώποις. I shall discuss below (cf. pp. 92–8) the implications of the scholiast's other explanation of ἀγώνισμα as ὁ γλυκὺς λόγος.

Longus claims for his work τὸ τερπνόν and τὸ μυθῶδες which Thucydides rejected, but also τὸ ὠφέλιμον (Horace's *utile*) which the historian saw as the hallmark of his own work, κτῆμα … ὃ καὶ νοσοῦντα ἰάσεται καὶ λυπούμενον παραμυθήσεται, τὸν ἐρασθέντα ἀναμνήσει, τὸν οὐκ ἐρασθέντα προπαιδεύσει. Plato had banished 'sweet poetry' because it lacked this element of τὸ ὠφέλιμον (cf. *R.* 3.398a–b, 10.607d), but Longus' claim here is one which occurs often in ancient erotic literature, cf. Prop 1.7.13–14 *me legat assidue post haec neglectus amator,| et prosint illi cognita nostra mala*, 1.10.15–18, 3.3.47–50, Ovid, *Am.* 2.1.5–10, Philostr. *Epist.* 68 Benner–Fobes οἱ ἐρωτικοὶ τῶν ποιητῶν ἀγαθὴ ἀκρόασις καὶ ἐξώροις, ἄγουσι γὰρ αὐτοὺς εἰς ἔννοιαν τοῦ ἐρᾶν ὥσπερ ἀνηβηκότας … ἡ γὰρ συνουσία τῶν τοιῶνδε ποιητῶν ἢ οὐκ ἐπιλήσει σε ἀφροδισίων ἢ ἀναμνήσει.[107] That poetry can cure the νόσος of love is an idea that Longus would have found in Theocritus, *Idyll* 11 (cf. vv. 1–3 which are echoed at *D&C* 2.7.7, v. 17, vv. 80–1, Call. *Epigr.* 46 Pf. = *HE* 1047). At a less literary level the doctor Theodorus Priscianus (late fourth or early fifth century A.D.) recommended the reading of love romances as a cure for impotence in males.[108] It was thus easy for Longus to find in the tradition a 'practical use' for his novel. We can also see here an example of the confluence of two major influences on *D&C*, the rhetorical tradition and the tradition of erotic literature. Seiler noted that Longus' claim is reminiscent of the story found at [Plut.] *Mor.* 833c–d and Philostr. *Vit.Soph.* 498 that Antiphon, the famous sophist of the fifth century B.C., consoled and cured the grief-stricken (οἱ λυπούμενοι) through the power of his so-called νηπενθεῖς ἀκροάσεις which he delivered in a special building in Corinth, and more generally we may remember Gorgias' claim for the power of λόγος, δύναται ... καὶ φόβον παῦσαι καὶ λύπην ἀφελεῖν καὶ χαρὰν ἐνεργάσασθαι καὶ ἔλεον ἐπαυξῆσαι (*Helen* 8).[109] It would be unsurprising if Longus harked back to the example of these great figures, but he may also have had a more contemporary inspiration. Under the emperor Julian, Zeno of Cyprus founded a school of medicine which laid as much stress upon persuasive powers of public speaking as upon medical knowledge;[110] his pupils expounded their theories in public lectures and one of them, Magnus of Nisibis, who was particuarly successful in Alexandria (cf. Eunapius, *Vit.Soph.* 498 = XX Giangrande), is almost certainly the man called an ἰατροσοφιστής by the Byzantine doctor Theophilus.[111] The links between philosophy, rhetoric and medicine are clearly to be seen already in the first and second centuries A.D.,[112] and so Longus may be seen to be drawing upon a tradition of 'sophistic medicine', a tradition which gives one more resonance to his self-advertisement in the prologue. The claim to cure love-sickness is no small thing, as most of antiquity recognised love as one νόσος over which doctors had no power.

To sum up this discussion: by presenting his novel as the story behind a painting which he had come across while hunting, Longus foreshadows the themes of art, nature and imitation which are to dominate the novel. This device also advertises the finite time-scale of the work and calls attention to its visual power. Moreover, in stressing his work's fictional nature and its academic affiliations within the long-established division of literature into the *dulce* and the *utile*, Longus lays playful claim to both of these virtues. In the prologue, therefore, the literary and rhetorical traditions are masterfully blended into an amusing and original form.

(v) The included narratives

In each of the first three books a brief mythological narrative is related; in Books 1 and 3 Daphnis tells Chloe a story of metamorphosis and in Book 2 Lamon tells Daphnis and Chloe a similar tale.[113] It may be helpful to set the passages out in full:

ἔτερψεν αὐτούς ποτε φάττα βουκολικὸν ἐκ τῆς ὕλης φθεγξαμένη, καὶ τῆς Χλόης ζητούσης μαθεῖν ὅ, τι λέγει διδάσκει αὐτὴν ὁ Δάφνις μυθολογῶν τὰ θρυλούμενα· 'ἦν παρθένος, παρθένε, οὕτω καλὴ καὶ ἔνεμε βοῦς πολλὰς οὕτως ἐν ὕλῃ. ἦν δὲ ἄρα καὶ ᾠδική, καὶ ἐτέρποντο αἱ βόες αὐτῆς τῆι μουσικῆι, καὶ ἔνεμεν οὔτε καλαύροπος πληγῆι οὔτε κέντρου προσβολῆι, ἀλλὰ καθίσασα ὑπὸ πίτυν καὶ στεφανωσαμένη πίτυι ἦιδε Πᾶνα καὶ τὴν Πίτυν, καὶ αἱ βόες τῆι φωνῆι παρέμενον. παῖς οὐ μακρὰν νέμων βοῦς, καὶ αὐτὸς καλὸς καὶ ᾠδικὸς ὡς ἡ παρθένος, φιλονεικήσας πρὸς τὴν μελωιδίαν μείζονα ὡς ἀνήρ, ἡδεῖαν ὡς παῖς φωνὴν ἀντεπεδείξατο καὶ τῶν βοῶν ὀκτὼ τὰς ἀρίστας ἐς τὴν ἰδίαν ἀγέλην θέλξας ἀπεβουκόλησεν. ἄχθεται ἡ παρθένος τῆι βλάβηι τῆς ἀγέλης, τῆι ἥττηι τῆς ὠιδῆς, καὶ εὔχεται τοῖς θεοῖς ὄρνις γενέσθαι πρὶν οἴκαδε ἀφικέσθαι. πείθονται οἱ θεοὶ καὶ ποιοῦσι τήνδε τὴν ὄρνιν, ὄρειον ὡς ἡ παρθένος, μουσικὴν ὡς ἐκείνη, καὶ ἔτι νῦν ἄιδουσα μηνύει τὴν συμφοράν, ὅτι βοῦς ζητεῖ πεπλανημένας.'

(1.27)

ὁ δὲ Λάμων ἐπηγγείλατο αὐτοῖς τὸν περὶ τῆς σύριγγος ἀφηγήσασθαι μῦθον, ὃν αὐτῶι Σικελὸς αἰπόλος ἦισεν ἐπὶ μισθῶι τράγωι καὶ σύριγγι· 'αὕτη ἡ σῦριγξ τὸ ἀρχαῖον οὐκ ἦν ὄργανον ἀλλὰ παρθένος καλὴ καὶ τὴν φωνὴν μουσική. αἶγας ἔνεμε, Νύμφαις συνέπαιζεν, ἦιδεν οἷον νῦν. Πὰν ταύτης νεμούσης, παιζούσης, ἀιδούσης προσελθὼν ἔπειθεν ἐς ὅ, τι ἐχρῆιζε καὶ ἐπηγγέλλετο τὰς αἶγας πάσας θήσειν διδυμοτόκους. ἡ δὲ ἐγέλα τὸν ἔρωτα αὐτοῦ οὐδὲ ἐραστὴν ἔφη δέξεσθαι μήτε τράγον μήτε ἄνθρωπον ὁλόκληρον, ὁρμᾶι διώκειν ὁ Πὰν ἐς βίαν. ἡ Σῦριγξ ἔφευγε καὶ τὸν Πᾶνα καὶ τὴν βίαν, φεύγουσα κάμνουσα ἐς δόνακας κρύπτεται, εἰς ἕλος ἀφανίζεται. Πὰν τοὺς δόνακας ὀργῆι τεμὼν τὴν κόρην οὐχ εὑρὼν τὸ πάθος μαθὼν τὸ ὄργανον νοεῖ καὶ τοὺς καλάμους

⟨ἐμπνεῖ⟩ [suppl. Reeve] κηρῶι συνδήσας ἀνίσους καθότι καὶ ὁ ἔρως
ἄνισος αὐτοῖς· καὶ ἡ τότε παρθένος καλὴ νῦν ἐστὶ σῦριγξ μουσική.'

(2.33.3–34)

'Νυμφῶν, ὦ κόρη, πολὺ γένος, Μελίαι καὶ Δρυάδες καὶ Ἕλειοι, πᾶσαι
καλαί, πᾶσαι μουσικαί. μιᾶς τούτων θυγάτηρ Ἠχὼ γίνεται, θνητὴ μὲν
ὡς ἐκ πατρὸς θνητοῦ, καλὴ δὲ ὡς ἐκ μητρὸς καλῆς. τρέφεται μὲν ὑπὸ
Νυμφῶν, παιδεύεται δὲ ὑπὸ Μουσῶν συρίζειν, αὐλεῖν, τὰ πρὸς λύραν,
τὰ πρὸς κιθάραν, πᾶσαν ὠιδήν· ὥστε καὶ παρθενίας εἰς ἄνθος ἀκμάσασα
ταῖς Νύμφαις συνεχόρευε, ταῖς Μούσαις συνῆιδεν. ἄρρενας δὲ ἔφευγε
πάντας, καὶ ἀνθρώπους καὶ θεούς, φιλοῦσα τὴν παρθενίαν. ὁ Πὰν
ὀργίζεται τῆι κόρηι, τῆς μουσικῆς φθονῶν, τοῦ κάλλους μὴ τυχών,
καὶ μανίαν ἐμβάλλει τοῖς ποιμέσι καὶ τοῖς αἰπόλοις· οἱ δὲ ὥσπερ κύνες
ἢ λύκοι διασπῶσιν αὐτὴν καὶ ῥίπτουσιν εἰς πᾶσαν τὴν γῆν ἔτι ἄιδοντα
τὰ μέλη, καὶ τὰ μέλη Γῆ χαριζομένη Νύμφαις ἔκρυψε πάντα καὶ ἐτήρησε
τὴν μουσικὴν καὶ γνώμηι Μουσῶν ἀφίησι φωνὴν καὶ μιμεῖται πάντα
καθάπερ τότε ἡ κόρη, θεούς, ἀνθρώπους, ὄργανα, θηρία· μιμεῖται
καὶ αὐτὸν συρίττοντα τὸν Πᾶνα, ὁ δὲ ἀκούσας ἀναπηδᾶι καὶ διώκει
κατὰ τῶν ὀρῶν οὐκ ἐρῶν τυχεῖν ἀλλ' ἢ τοῦ μαθεῖν τίς ἐστιν ὁ
λανθάνων μαθητής.'

(3.23)

It is at once clear that there are various patterns in these
stories: in each music has an important role and in each there
is an erotic (or anti-erotic) element; in the first story *eros*
appears in the reference to the love of Pan for Pitys, in the
second Syrinx seems to be a normal girl who would have
been prepared to accept a fully human lover and in the third
Echo is a chaste maiden in the mould of Artemis. Similarly,
the violence and menace of the stories increases: in the first
story violence is only hinted at in the legend of Pan and
Pitys, if indeed Longus wishes ús to think of the story not
found in detail before the Byzantine period (cf. *Geoponica*
11.10) in which Pitys was horribly killed by Pan's rival
Boreas,[114] i.e. a story in which Pan lost his love through no
fault of his own. In the story of Syrinx Pan unwittingly kills
his beloved, and in the story of Echo Pan deliberately
destroys the girl in a most savage way. In this last story, the
σπαραγμός of Echo, which is a version found to my knowledge nowhere else, is clearly a 'Dionysiac element' in the
novel; more specifically, we are reminded of the fate of
Orpheus who was torn apart by Thracian maenads and whose

head, still singing, floated to Lesbos where it was buried at a spot which became a shrine and oracle.[115] The traditional story of Orpheus and the Longan story of Echo both proclaim the power of music over the forces of destruction, a theme with wide ramifications in the novel as a whole. I have considered elsewhere (cf. above pp. 30-1) the 'identification' of Daphnis with Orpheus in certain episodes of the novel.

Longus has pointed to the links between these stories and the story of Daphnis and Chloe in various ways. In the story of the φάττα Daphnis' opening words link Chloe to the heroine of the myth, ἦν παρθένος, παρθένε, οὕτω καλή κτλ., and the girl's crown of pine (1.27.2) recalls Chloe's similar headwear in 1.24.1; immediately after the story of Syrinx the children repeat the story in mime, thus making clear the identification already hinted at in the girl's connection with the Nymphs and Pan's attempts at persuasion; in the story of Echo the fact that the girl was reared by the Nymphs and that in his anger Pan cast a frenzy 'on the shepherds and goatherds' recalls Chloe's upbringing and the effect of her beauty on the people of the countryside (cf. 2.2.2) and, in particular, on Daphnis. It may, further, be worth recalling that in their hurried conversation in the depths of winter Chloe had answered Daphnis καθάπερ ἠχώ (3.11.1).

Metamorphosis had long been a theme of bucolic poetry (Bion, *Lament for Adonis* 37-43, V. *Ecl.* 6) but the place of these stories in the main narrative is not easy to determine with any precision, although it is clear that as these μῦθοι mirror, however dimly, the story of Daphnis and Chloe, they help to establish the status of the novel itself as a μῦθος. It is perhaps obvious that the increasing savagery of the three stories foreshadows the loss of Chloe's virginity, which draws ever closer, and that the story of Echo in particular emphasises that although first sex will be, as Lycaenion describes it, 'bloody', a refusal to yield would have even more disastrous consequences. We ought not to miss, however, the typically Longan irony with which Daphnis grows less rather than more insistent as time goes on, whereas Chloe shows no obvious reluctance to yield to 'the forces of nature' (cf. 3.24.3). Violence and desecration recall the garden of Lamon which is described in great detail at the opening of Book 4 and which is ruined by Lampis in 4.7 in an attempt to turn Dionysophanes against Daphnis. The link between wonderful gardens and women or *eros* in general is familiar from Homer onwards (cf. Calypso, *Od.* 5.63–75 and Nausicaa, *Od.* 7.112–32)[116] and has a particularly prominent place in the novel of Achilles Tatius and in the later Byzantine novels.[117] The desecration of Lamon's garden by a man acting ὥσπερ σῦς cannot simply represent the violence of love as we see it in the defloration of Chloe, as the gulf between the seriousness of Lampis' actions and the grief they cause on one hand and the eagerness with which Chloe embraces her fate on the other would make this symbolism almost impossibly humorous, even for Longus. There are at least two other factors involved here also. One is the simple fact that this deed characterises Lampis as so unlike Daphnis as to be quite unworthy of Chloe; the love that both Dorcon and Lampis try to force upon Chloe, like that which Gnathon offers to Daphnis (cf. below p. 71) and Pan to Echo, is rape, whereas Daphnis' love is one of mutual affection and gentle persuasion. Secondly, it is easy enough to see in the desecration of the garden the new life which Daphnis and Chloe are about to encounter and, more particularly, the dangerously perverse and urban threat which Gnathon poses. In this latter case we smile again as we look back at the gulf between the high art of the θρῆνος (4.8.3–4) and the actual danger which threatens Daphnis; we never really worry that Gnathon will get his hands on 'our hero' and only boys of fifteen (who did not, in my view, form a significant element of Longus' readership) might find the events of 4.12 fraught with suspense and danger. As for the link between Lamon's garden and the bucolic world in general,[118] we must not view the novel in terms of a black-and-white opposition between Town and Country. The ending of the novel suggests rather a balance between the two — although the children are partially drawn into the urban world, their pastoral life continues.

Beyond the superficial differences of food (4.15.4) and smell
(4.38.4) – and the novelty of Gnathon's sexual tastes – there
is no fundamental gulf between the two worlds: both are full
of people trying to steer a path through life's hazards.

Of the three included myths it is that of the φάττα which
is most closely tied to the surrounding events in the novel.
The boy and the girl of the story obviously remind us of
Daphnis and Chloe (although Daphnis is a goatherd and not,
as the boy in the story, a cowherd), and, as critics have
realised,[119] the fact that the girl is destroyed by the boy's
musical skill looks forward to the following events where
the reverse happens when Chloe saves Daphnis by playing
upon Dorcon's pipes. Although this story of the φάττα
contains many familiar folk-tale motifs[120] and Longus
introduces it as τὰ θρυλούμενα, it does not, to my knowledge, occur elsewhere in ancient literature and it may be
largely Longus' own work,[121] just as Longus also revised
the traditional story of Echo to suit his own purposes (cf.
above pp. 53–4). The story of the φάττα is particularly successful because the lack of any explicitly erotic relationship
between the boy and the girl gives peculiar force to the hints
that we are in fact to see *eros* at work here also. The φάττα
is found as a love-gift in Theocritus (5.96, 133), and so too
the tale may be seen as a pledge from Daphnis to Chloe;
secondly, the loss that the παρθένος suffers, and her subsequent sorrow, may make us think of what a παρθένος
normally loses when she meets a παῖς and of the sorrow
which traditionally attends such a loss (cf. Sappho fr. 114
LP–V). It is, moreover, important that the story of the
φάττα follows immediately upon the episode of the τέττιξ
in which Daphnis plays a far from innocent role, προφάσεως
λαβόμενος καθῆκεν αὐτῆς εἰς τὰ στέρνα τὰς χεῖρας καὶ
ἐξάγει τὸν βέλτιστον τέττιγα (1.26.3).[122] The story in Plato's
Phaedrus of the men who were so besotted with the pleasure
of music that they wasted away to become τέττιγες who eat
nothing and sing all day (259b–c) is one of the examples
chosen by Hermogenes to illustrate the 'sweet' qualities of
myths (cf. below p. 96). The Platonic myth lacks, however,

the erotic undertone of the story of the φάττα, and Longus may also have preferred not to use a myth as well known as Plato's story of the τέττιξ which seemed to offer little scope for innovation. That the Platonic myth was indeed in Longus' mind when composing this episode is perhaps suggested by the fact that Chloe has been lulled to sleep in the midday heat while Daphnis pipes and her flocks rest in the shade; in the *Phaedrus* Socrates tells Phaedrus that they must not be lulled to sleep by the music of the cicadas (ἐν μεσημβρίαι . . . νυστάζοντας καὶ κηλουμένους ὑπ' αὐτῶν, cf. *D&C* 1.25.1) lest these creatures consider them no better than sheep sleeping around a spring at midday (*Phdr.* 259a). Both the men in Plato's story and Longus' παρθένος received the gift of rustic music from the gods, but whereas the τέττιγες are perfectly happy with their lot, the παρθένος is still searching for something which only a παῖς can give her. Finally, the protection which Daphnis and Chloe give to the τέττιξ is a clear sign of their piety and of the happiness which awaits them, if we remember the special role as divine spies which Plato allots to the τέττιγες (*Phdr.* 259c–d): there is no doubt that Daphnis and Chloe honour Erato throughout the novel ἐν τοῖς ἐρωτικοῖς and that the τέττιξ will give a very good report of them to the Muses.

(vi) *Conclusion*

It will by now be clear that I consider among the greatest attractions of *D&C* the very light touch with which Longus picks up and lets go all forms of literary and intellectual pretension and the skill with which this apparently simple tale seems to suggest layer after layer of meaning and resonance. These features of *D&C* are particularly noticeable, as I have sought to demonstrate, in the prologue, where the knowledge of the rhetorical and literary traditions which we bring to our reading helps us to appreciate how Longus amusingly undercuts the apparent earnestness of his claims, in the included mythological narratives which stimulate us because they suggest the story of the main narrative to us, but do so obliquely, and in the novel's presentation of divine forces which are both the banal figures of later Greek literature and the primal currents of nature.

There is, of course, no necessary divorce between high artifice and real intellectual depth, and we are lucky that some ancient writers who exhibit both characteristics survive. Longus is not to be numbered in their company, because he tickles rather than nourishes our intellects. This is, however, no mean service, particularly when it is set against much else that survives from the Greek literature of the imperial period.

CHAPTER THREE

THE LITERARY TEXTURE

D&C is replete with echoes of and allusions to archaic, classical and Hellenistic Greek literature.[1] As with any work which draws heavily upon earlier literature, there are cases where it can be argued that the debt is unconscious,[2] or that it serves no function beyond a purely ornamental one, and other cases where it may be disputed whether the debt is specifically to one ancestor or simply a general reflection of a widespread tradition.[3] In the majority of cases, however, an echo of earlier literature invests a scene with a layer of meaning which would otherwise be difficult to fit into the artificially simple narrative; it allows the author to direct a reader's reaction without in fact having to intrude directly into the narrative. Thus, for example, when at 2.23.4 the Nymphs tell Daphnis in a dream that he is to receive martial assistance from Pan to whom Daphnis and Chloe have never shown the slightest honour, we think of Pan's reproof and promise to the Athenians which he delivered to the runner Philippides on the Arcadian plain at the time of the Persian invasion (Hdt. 6.105).[4] This echo not only emphasises that justice is on Daphnis' side against the Methymnaeans, but also points to the amusing distance between the great events of Herodotus' history and the small world which Daphnis and Chloe inhabit. No 'formula' will fit every case, and in the first part of this chapter I wish simply to illustrate some of the ways in which Longus exploits the two authors from whom he has borrowed most, Homer and Theocritus.[5] This latter debt is acknowledged at 2.33.3 where Lamon says that he learned the story of Syrinx from a Σικελὸς αἰπόλος: this must be both a compliment to Theocritus (to whom the 'figure-poem' *Syrinx* was ascribed in antiquity) and a reference to the fact that the invention of bucolic poetry (for which the syrinx is a standard symbol) was placed by most ancient scholars in Sicily.[6]

Longus shares with much Hellenistic and later literature the practice of preserving creative independence by changing the features of a literary model or by combining two or more different models. Thus, for example, Philetas' description of Eros at 2.6.1, ἀνήλατο καθάπερ ἀηδόνος νεοττὸς ἐπὶ τὰς μυρρίνας καὶ κλάδον ἀμείβων ἐκ κλάδου διὰ τῶν φύλλων ἀνεῖρπεν εἰς ἄκρον, seems to combine Theocr. 15.120-2,

οἱ δέ τε κῶροι ὑπερπωτῶνται Ἔρωτες
οἷοι ἀηδονιδῆες ἀεξομενᾶν ἐπὶ δένδρωι
πωτῶνται πτερύγων πειρώμενοι ὄζον ἀπ' ὄζω,

with Theocr. 29.14-15,

νῦν δὲ τῶδε μὲν ἄματος ἄλλον ἔχηις κλάδον,
ἄλλον δ' αὔριον, ἐξ ἀτέρω δ' ἄτερον μάτης,

within a description borrowed from a poem of Bion about Eros as a bird (cf. pp. 77-8).[7] Similarly, 4.14.2, εἴ ποτε Ἀπόλλων Λαομέδοντι θητεύων ἐβουκόλησε, τοιόσδε ἦν οἷος τότε ὤφθη Δάφνις, lightly echoes Poseidon's speech at Il. 21.441-9 (cf. v. 444 θητεύσαμεν, v. 448 βουκολέεσκες) while changing the syntax of the original. At 2.5.3 the phrase τὸ πλατὺ βουκόλιον is modelled on the epic phrase αἰπόλια πλατέ' αἰγῶν (Hom. Il. 2.474, 11.679, Od. 14.101-3, Hes. Theog. 445), but Longus has changed plural to singular and used the expression of cattle rather than goats.[8] At 3.3.4, τότε βοῶν ἐπὶ φάτναις φροντὶς ἦν ἄχυρον ἐσθιόντων, αἰγῶν καὶ προβάτων ἐν τοῖς σηκοῖς φυλλάδας, ὑῶν ἐν τοῖς συφεοῖς ἄκυλον καὶ βαλάνους, Longus uses the Homeric phrase βοῦς ἐπὶ φάτνηι (Od. 4.535, 11.411),[9] with grammatical (plural for singular) and syntactic alteration, and also exploits another Homeric passage, Od. 10.241-3 τοῖσι δὲ Κίρκη | πάρ ῥ' ἄκυλον βάλανόν τε βάλεν καρπόν τε κρανείης | ἔδμεναι, οἷα σύες χαμαιευνάδες αἰὲν ἔδουσιν.

In some cases the original context of a borrowed phrase is particularly important. At 3.15.2 we learn that Lycaenion was attracted to Daphnis when she saw him καθ' ἑκάστην ἡμέραν παρελαύνοντα τὰς αἶγας ἕωθεν εἰς νομήν, νύκτωρ ἐκ νομῆς; the situation here is that of Theocr. 5.88-9 where Comatas claims that Clearista makes sexual overtures to him, βάλλει καὶ μάλοισι τὸν αἰπόλον ἀ Κλεαρίστα | τὰς αἶγας παρελᾶντα καὶ ἀδύ τι ποππυλιάσδει, and note also Daphnis' claim at Theocr. 8.72-3, κἤμ' ἐκ τῶ ἄντρω σύνοφρυς κόρα ἐχθὲς ἰδοῖσα | τὰς δαμάλας παρελᾶντα καλὸν καλὸν ἦμεν ἔφασκεν. Gnathon, who presents a sexual challenge of a different kind from Lycaenion, is linked to her by a similar echo, cf. 4.12.1 νύκτωρ λοχήσας ἐκ τῆς νομῆς ἐλαύνοντα [sc. τὸν Δάφνιν] τὰς αἶγας πρῶτον μὲν ἐφίλησε προσδραμών, εἶτα ἔπειθε παρασχεῖν τοιοῦτον οἷον αἱ αἶγες τοῖς τράγοις. An allusion to earlier literature is often used to create a humorous or ironic atmosphere. It is, for example, amusing that Lycaenion's story about the loss of one of her twenty geese (3.16.2) echoes Penelope's prophetic dream which she recounts to Odysseus at *Od.* 19.536-53. In the matter of marital fidelity Lycaenion and Penelope are at opposite ends of the spectrum. When Longus compares the farmers as they attack the Methymnaeans to ψᾶρες ἢ κολοιοί (2.17.3) he is echoing *Il.* 17.755 where the Achaeans who flee before Hector and Aeneas are compared to a ψαρῶν νέφος . . . ἠὲ κολοιῶν which flees at the sight of a hawk. Here the humour comes not so much from the contrast between the heroic world and the world of the novel, but rather from the amused condescension with which the author treats his characters. At 1.28.2 the Tyrian pirates capture Daphnis ἀλύοντα περὶ[10] τὴν θάλασσαν. The motif here is derived from the *Homeric Hymn to Dionysus* in which the λῃστοὶ Τυρσηνοί capture the handsome young god παρὰ θῖν' ἁλὸς ἀτρυγέτοιο (vv. 2-3), but we are surely also intended to remember how at *Il.* 24.12 the distraught Achilles δινεύεσκ' ἀλύων παρὰ θῖν' ἁλός. Here the contrast between Daphnis and Achilles is lightly amusing and Longus has varied his model by using ἀλύειν in its later sense of 'wander aimlessly' rather than 'be distraught'.[11] A similar, though less certain, case occurs at 1.30.4-5 where the account of Daphnis' rescue from shipwreck, pulled to shore by two powerfully swimming oxen (a miracle that reminds us of the rescue of another famous Lesbian musician, Arion, who fell into the hands of some wicked sailors and was carried to safety on the back of a dolphin), may echo Odysseus' rescue at *Od.* 5.370-5; in Homer Odysseus saves himself as the ship shatters by climbing on to a plank, κέληθ' ὡς ἵππον ἐλαύνων, and then stripping off his clothes, whereas Daphnis first takes off his clothing and then scrambles on to his 'vessel' which he rides ὥσπερ ἐλαύνων ἄμαξαν. The changes in the order of events and from horse to wagon would be very much in Longus' style.[12] Finally, I note two cases where the fact that his characters are rustics allows Longus to use poetic quotation to pleasant effect. At 1.17.3 the effect on Daphnis of Chloe's kiss is described, τότε πρῶτον καὶ τὴν κόμην αὐτῆς ἐθαύμασεν ὅτι ξανθὴ καὶ τοὺς ὀφθαλμοὺς ὅτι μεγάλοι καθάπερ βοὸς καὶ τὸ πρόσωπον ὅτι λευκότερον ἀληθῶς καὶ τοῦ τῶν αἰγῶν γάλακτος, ὥσπερ τότε πρῶτον ὀφθαλμοὺς κτησάμενος, τὸν δὲ πρότερον χρόνον πεπηρωμένος. The echo of the epic epithet βοῶπις is appropriate here because Daphnis is one person who would know what the eyes of a βοῦς look like. For the reference to the whiteness of Chloe's face Longus is presumably indebted to Theocr. 11.19-21,

> ὦ λευκὰ Γαλάτεια, τί τὸν φιλέοντ' ἀποβάλληι,
> λευκοτέρα πακτᾶς ποτιδεῖν, ἀπαλωτέρα ἀρνός,
> μόσχω γαυροτέρα, φιαρωτέρα ὄμφακος ὠμᾶς;

(For Daphnis as the Cyclops cf. below p. 63). Longus may also have been familiar with the archaic poetry which lies behind this passage of Theocritus, cf. Greg. Cor. *in Hermog. Meth.* 13 (*Rhet.Gr.* 7.1236 Walz) αἰσχρῶς μὲν κολακεύει τὴν ἀκοὴν ἐκεῖνα, ὅσα εἰσὶν ἐρωτικά, οἷον τὰ Ἀνακρέοντος (*PMG* 488 = fr. 173 Gentili), τὰ Σαπφοῦς (fr. 156 LP-V), οἷον γάλακτος λευκοτέρα, ὕδατος ἀπαλωτέρα, πηκτίδων ἐμμελεστέρα, ἵππου γαυροτέρα, ῥόδων ἀβροτέρα, ἱματίου ἐανοῦ μαλακωτέρα, χρυσοῦ τιμιωτέρα. The distribution of these phrases between Anacreon and Sappho[13] is less important than the fact that in *D&C* we are to recognise in λευκότερον ἀληθῶς καὶ τοῦ τῶν αἰγῶν γάλακτος a poetic quotation and realise that it has been made particularly appropriate to its new context by the added specification 'goat's milk'; ἀληθῶς points to the fact that this is not simply an ornamental echo. The effect is humorous in precisely the same way as Theocritus' more concise λευκοτέρα πακτᾶς. At 1.18.1 Longus is presumably thinking of the same models again, χείλη μὲν ῥόδων ἁπαλώτερα καὶ στόμα κηρίων γλυκύτερον.[14] It is perhaps worth noting here that in the passage which I have quoted Gregory is commenting upon Hermogenes' discussion (p. 429.10 R) of sophistic jingles and the excessive use of parisa, and that after citing 'Sappho' and 'Anacreon' Gregory adduces as examples of this style Achilles Tatius, Xenophon of Ephesus and τὰ ἄλλα ἐρωτικά. Here we can see clearly the link between style and subject in D&C which I shall investigate more fully elsewhere (cf. below pp. 90–1).

The second case to be considered under this head is a series of parallels between Daphnis and the Homeric and Theocritean Cyclops: 3.28.1 ὁ Δάφνις περιχαρὴς ἤλαυνε ῥοίζωι πολλῶι τὰς αἶγας εἰς τὴν νομήν (cf. 2.10.2) echoes Od. 9.315 πολλῆι δὲ ῥοίζωι πρὸς ὄρος τρέπε πίονα μῆλα| Κύκλωψ,[15] the list of milking equipment at 4.4.4 recalls Od. 9.219–23, and 3.33.2 where Daphnis helps Chloe with her chores after she has been promised in marriage to him, ἤμελγε μὲν εἰς γαυλοὺς τὸ γάλα, ἐνεπήγνυ δὲ ταρσοῖς τοὺς τυροὺς κτλ., echoes the picture of conjugal bliss which the Cyclops holds out to Galatea at Theocr. 11.65–6, ποιμαίνειν δ' ἐθέλοις σὺν ἐμὶν ἅμα καὶ γάλ' ἀμέλγειν| καὶ τυρὸν πᾶξαι τάμισον δριμεῖαν ἐνεῖσα.

In moving from isolated echoes to the borrowing of scenes and motifs it is natural to ask first whether the links which bind D&C to 'the Greek novel' are in fact as strong as the traditional scholarly classification would suggest. Like the novel of Achilles Tatius, D&C is a prose narrative about the adventures of a boy and a girl which culminates in their marriage (and, more importantly, first physical union); in the novels of Xenophon of Ephesus and Chariton the hero and heroine are separated after marriage and happily reunited at the end of the work, although this difference between these works is not of itself very significant. The 'happy ending' of D&C, as well as being what every reader expects, is explicitly forecast by Eros at 2.5.3–4 when he tells Philetas that he is looking after Daphnis and Chloe just as he cared for Philetas and Amaryllis who are now married with children of their own.[16] I shall return presently to the differences between *D&C* and the other prose narratives which survive, but it is to be noted at once that certain scenes resemble parallel scenes in other ancient novels in such a way as clearly to set *D&C* within the same tradition. The sequence at 2.22–3 in which Daphnis upbraids the Nymphs for allowing Chloe to be taken by the Methymnaeans and is then comforted by a prophetic dream finds a close parallel at Xen. Eph. 2.8, and Daphnis' lament has echoes throughout the extant romances (cf., eg., Ach. Tat. 3.10), as also does the motif of the dream (a comic example at Petr. *Sat.* 104). The reunions of Daphnis and Chloe at 2.30.2 and 3.7.3[17] are reminiscent of many similiarly happy events in these works (cf. Heliod. 2.6.3, Xen. Eph. 5.13.3), and Daphnis is threatened by rival suitors[18] and by a homosexual in a way which we recognise from the other novels (cf. Chariton 1.1.9, Xen. Eph. 1.14–15). Chloe is threatened by Dorcon and Lampis in the way that the heroines of the extant romances are habitually endangered, and 4.28 in which she is carried off by Lampis resembles the rapes of Cleitophon's sister and of Leucippe in Achilles (2.16–18, 6.4). The trial scene in 2.15–16 has parallels in Chariton and Achilles, but is particularly noteworthy for the high rhetorical artistry of Daphnis' speech which is in sharp contrast to the blunt statement (σαφῆ καὶ σύντομα 2.15.1) of the prosecuting Methymnaeans: ἀλλ' ἀπέφαγον τὴν λύγον. οὐ γὰρ εἶχον ἐν ψάμμωι πόαν ἢ κόμαρον ἢ θύμον. ἀλλ' ἀπώλετο ἡ ναῦς ὑπὸ τοῦ πνεύματος καὶ τῆς θαλάσσης. ταῦτα χειμῶνος οὐκ αἰγῶν ἐστιν ἔργα. ἀλλ' ἐσθὴς ἐνέκειτο καὶ ἄργυρος. καὶ τίς πιστεύσει νοῦν ἔχων ὅτι τοσαῦτα φέρουσα ναῦς πεῖσμα εἶχε λύγον;. After this trio of arguments (each introduced, in a favourite mannerism of orators,[19] by ἀλλά) has been swept away (the last by an argument from εἰκός, probability), Daphnis begins to weep to arouse pity in the time-honoured fashion of Athenian courts (2.17.1). This survey of the links between *D&C* and the other Greek novels

could be much extended, but I add only 4.33.3-4 in which
the coming marriage sets Mytilene alight, ὅλη . . . ἐκινεῖτο
ἡ πόλις ἐπὶ τῶι μειρακίωι καὶ τῆι παρθένωι; this motif is
a common one in the ancient love romances, cf. Xen. Eph.
1.7.3-4, *Hist.Apoll.Tyr.*23 and the following passage from
the scanty fragments of the *Romance of Chione*, ταχέως
δὲ διεφοίτησε ἀνὰ τὴν πόλιν ἅπασαν . . . φήμη καὶ οὐθεὶς
ἄλλο οὐδὲν ἐλάλει ἢ περὶ τοῦ γάμου (fr. 3 Lavagnini = 3.II
Zimmermann).[20]

It is thus clear that the links between *D&C* and the tradition of the prose romance are strong. Nevertheless, most
readers will feel that the differences between this work and
the other 'Greek novels' are at least as marked as are the
similarities. Longus' work is not simply a pastoral version of
the novel, although scholarship has been too often inclined
to treat it as such, presumably on the principle that what is
classified is also explained. It is, on the contrary, my impression that Longus does not seek to make any sustained capital
out of his readers' awareness that he is exploiting the tradition of prose romance (along with many other traditions),
and I would contrast the *Satyricon* of Petronius in which,
as Heinze and others have demonstrated,[21] the two 'heroes'
find themselves from time to time in situations reminiscent
of the 'ideal' romance and it is clear that Petronius has used
this likeness for humorous and sometimes parodic effects;
very much the same is true also of the novel of Achilles. In
D&C there is no such pointed use of the tradition, although
there are, as I have already noted, many common motifs
of the novel which appear in a 'bucolic guise'.[22] The essential
difference between *D&C* and the other works which are
normally lumped together as 'The Greek Novel' lies not in
the pastoral setting of the former, but rather in its conception and structure. Although Daphnis and Chloe move
inexorably towards union, this narrative thread takes second
place to the elaboration of incidents and scenes which are
virtually complete in themselves.[23] This episodic character
of the work is unmistakable and more clearly marked than in
the other Greek novels, although the actual division into

episodes may be a matter of dispute: in an influential article[24] O. Schissel proposed that *D&C* was divisible into twelve episodes (plus the proem) and that in each episode an introduction (often setting the time or place) was followed by a section devoted to Daphnis, then one to Chloe and then one in which the children are together. Although this attractively symmetrical scheme does in fact work for the opening section of the novel (1.1–8), it later breaks down or produces unnatural divisions and so cannot be accepted in its entirety.[25] Nevertheless, the essentially episodic nature of the novel is undisputed and the episodes are not, as they tend to be in the other novels, merely variations upon the theme of 'danger to the hero or heroine' but are, as the prologue suggested, discrete scenes drawn from a wide range of sources. Even in the matter of the 'love interest' *D&C* stands apart: the children are constantly together, although often separated for short periods by bad weather or pirates, and this gives an entirely different character to the main narrative.[26] Even without Longus' gently ironic attitude to his characters, we would care much less about the marriage of his two principals than we do in the other 'ideal' novels, simply because this marriage never seems in real doubt. The constant nearness of Daphnis and Chloe is comforting.

Another major element in Longus' work, the bucolic tradition, is most obvious to us in his borrowing from earlier bucolic poetry, but indications that he may also have exploited a tradition of bucolic prose fiction have been found in the seventh oration of Dio Chrysostom (the *Euboicus*), which tells how Dio was shipwrecked on the coast of Euboea and very hospitably entertained by some poor hunters.[27] Dio's purpose is, unlike Longus', an essentially moralising and exhortatory one,[28] but both writers draw upon traditional material about 'the simple countryside' and both are indebted to the rhetorical tradition in which σύγκρισις ἀγροῦ καὶ πόλεως, ἐγκώμιον γεωργίας and similar themes were standard subjects.[29] Particularly reminiscent of *D&C* is Dio's account of the shy love between the hunter's daughter and the son of another hunter (7.67–80), a section which concludes with a rustic wedding and in which the boy's claims to be considered worthy of the girl, καὶ ἔλαφον καταπονῶ καὶ σὺν ὑφίσταμαι. ὄψει δὲ αὔριον ἂν θέλῃς, ὦ ξένε. Καὶ τὸν λαγὼν τοῦτον σύ, ἔφην, ἔλαβες; Ἐγώ, ἔφη γελάσας κτλ. (7.71), remind us of Daphnis' speech in similar circumstances at 3.29.2 ἐγὼ καὶ θερίζειν [Kairis: συρίζειν codd.] οἶδα καλῶς καὶ κλᾶν ἄμπελον κτλ. Both Longus and Dio are skilful in ἠθοποιΐα, the presentation of convincing character (cf. Hermogenes pp. 20-2 R), and it is to be noted that the example which Hermogenes gives for an exercise in this skill has a bucolic flavour, τίνας ἂν εἴποι λόγους γεωργὸς πρῶτον ἰδὼν ναῦν (p. 21.12 R).[30] It is thus unnecessary to postulate a tradition of bucolic prose fiction outside the confines of the rhetorical schools in order to explain the similarities between Dio and Longus, but it is as well always to reflect upon how much ancient literature has been lost and the ways in which this loss distorts our view.

D&C has very strong and clear links with New Comedy.[31] It is well known that the ancients classified fictional prose narratives as δράματα and that the novelists themselves frequently use the language of the theatre in referring to the action of their works.[32] The motif of the exposure of children and their subsequent recognition through γνωρίσματα was considered a specifically dramatic and particularly comic motif.[33] In his account in 4.35 of how he came to expose Chloe, Megacles[34] says that he used up what little wealth he had in public services, εἰς χορηγίας καὶ τριηραρχίας,[35] and was thus unable to bring up a daughter; although economic factors must have very often influenced the exposure of children in the second century no less than in earlier ages, Megacles' story may remind us of Pataicus' account in Menander's Periceiromene of how sudden poverty caused him to lessen his financial burdens by exposing his baby daughter (vv. 802-12), a tale which also recalls Dionysophanes' story of how one day's bad luck robbed him of two of the three children who were left after he had exposed Daphnis (4.24.2). Even more striking than this is the similarity between the plot of D&C as a whole and the following account of a tragedy (probably the *Tyro* of Sophocles)[36] by a character in the *Epitrepontes* of Menander:

τεθέασαι τραγωιδούς, οἶδ᾽ ὅτι,
καὶ ταῦτα κατέχεις πάντα. Νηλέα τινα
Πελίαν τ᾽ ἐκείνους εὗρε πρεσβύτης ἀνὴρ
αἰπόλος, ἔχων οἵαν ἐγὼ νῦν διφθέραν,
ὡς δ᾽ ἤισθετ᾽ αὐτοὺς ὄντας αὐτοῦ κρείττονας,
λέγει τὸ πρᾶγμ᾽, ὡς εὗρεν, ὡς ἀνείλετο.
ἔδωκε δ᾽ αὐτοῖς πηρίδιον γνωρισμάτων,
ἐξ οὗ μαθόντες πάντα τὰ καθ᾽ αὐτοὺς σαφῶς
ἐγένοντο βασιλεῖς οἱ τότ᾽ ὄντες αἰπόλοι. (*Epitr.* 325-33)

This tragic plot is used by Menander as a paradigm for the comic story which the audience is watching. The Menandrean character then mentions plays in which recognition tokens have prevented a brother marrying his sister, and I would suggest that Longus teases us with the possibility that Daphnis and Chloe will turn out to be siblings. Their lack of success in love-making perhaps hints at this ending, as does Lamon's suggestion at 3.31.4, νῦν δὲ φιλείτωσαν ἀλλήλους ὡς ἀδελφοί. Moreover, the name of the nurse who exposed Daphnis, Σωφροσύνη (or, with Courier's correction, Σωφρόνη),[37] is also the name of nurses in the *Eunuchus* and *Phormio* of Terence and in a letter of Aristaenetus (1.6) who borrows freely from the New Comedy. It is indeed in certain of his characters that Longus reminds us most of the New Comedy. Although the scene of love-making between Daphnis and Lycaenion and their subsequent conversation are hard to imagine in a play of the New Comedy, the character of Lycaenion does seem to have links with the 'kind-hearted' courtesans familiar from the dramatic genre. It is interesting that although her name most immediately suggests a connection with prostitution and loose morals[38] — Propertius tells us that he too lost his virginity to a girl called Lycinna (3.15)[39] — τὸ λυκαίνιον was the name given to a comic mask worn by a γράιδιον ἰσχνόν (Pollux 4.150). Lycaenion is no γράιδιον ἰσχνόν, but the link with the theatre was sufficient for Longus' purposes: with this name he could express more than one side of the character of

Chromis' wife. The links between this character and Comedy are strengthened by the fact that the excuse which Lycaenion uses to get out of the house (3.16.1) is the same as that used by Praxagora at Ar. *Eccl.* 528-9 (cf. above pp. 11-12). Her name also links Lycaenion to Dorcon who in the disguise of a wolf sought to ambush Chloe in the first book; happily, however, Lycaenion's 'attack' upon Daphnis is markedly more successful than Dorcon's on Chloe.

Both Dionysophanes' son Astylus and the latter's parasite Gnathon have links with New Comedy. Astylus, πλούσιος νεανίσκος καὶ τρυφῶν ἀεὶ καὶ ἀφιγμένος εἰς τὸν ἀγρὸν εἰς ἀπόλαυσιν ξένης ἡδονῆς (4.11.1), reminds us of the idle Sostratus in Menander's *Dyscolus*, a young man, ἀστικὸς τῆι διατριβῆι (v. 41), who has nothing better to do than fall in love while hunting in the countryside;[40] the difference between the urban and rural view of the countryside is well expressed at 4.5.2 where the peasants hurry on with their work ὡς εἴη καὶ τοῖς ἐκ τῆς πόλεως ἐλθοῦσιν ἐν εἰκόνι καὶ ἡδονῆι γενέσθαι τρυγητοῦ.[41] The parasite bears a name familiar from both New Comedy itself (Men. *Kolax*, Ter. *Eunuchus*) and later literature (Plut. *Mor.* 707e, Lucian, *Drap.* 19, *Timon* 45, Alc. 2.32, 3.8, Hesychius γ 705 Latte)[42] as a standard name for such a character. The similarity between 4.16.4 ξιφίδιον λαβὼν καὶ ἐμπλήσας τὴν γαστέρα τροφῆς ἐμαυτὸν ἀποκτενῶ πρὸ τῶν Δάφνιδος θυρῶν[43] and Alciphron 3.3.3 ἔκρινα οὖν πολυτελοῦς τραπέζης ἀπολαύσας ἀποπτύσαι τὸ ζῆν and 3.13.3 οὐ πρότερον στραγγαλιῶ τὸν τράχηλον πρὶν τραπέζης ἀπολαῦσαι παντελῶς suggests that both authors are drawing upon material from Comedy (although a common model is unlikely), and Gelasimus' final words in Plautus' *Stichus* (vv. 638-40) have a similar feel, while making a somewhat different point:

numquam edepol me uiuom quisquam in crastinum inspiciet diem;
nam mihi iam intus potione iuncea onerabo gulam,
neque ego hoc committam, ut me esse homines mortuum dicant fame.[44]

Our present corpus of New Comedy does not happen to contain a lovesick parasite, but such a character would not be improbable in drama, as comic poets liked to combine character types into new patterns — cf. the lovesick slave of Menander's *Heros* and Plautus' *Persa* — and in one of Alciphron's *Letters of parasites* we are presented with a parasite who falls in love with a girl whom he sees in a procession (3.31): his exclamation, αἰαῖ τῆς ἀγερωχίας, νῦν ἐμὲ μὴ ἐπιθυμεῖν θέρμων ἢ κυάμων ἢ ἀθάρας, ἀλλ' οὕτως ὑπερμαζᾶν καὶ τῶν ἀνεφίκτων ἐρᾶν, reminds us of Gnathon's confession of despair at 4.16.2 and it seems likely again that both writers are here drawing upon Comedy (cf. Men. *Mis.* 262–3 εἰ μὴ γὰρ οὗτος δοκιμάσει με, κυρίως | δώσει τε ταύτην, οἴχεται Θρασωνίδης).

It is, however, perhaps unlikely (although not impossible) that Longus found in New Comedy a parasite with strong homosexual preferences; there are in Roman Comedy two places where a joke is made about the bisexual tastes of a *miles gloriosus* who is attended by a parasite (Plaut. *MG* 1111–13 and Ter. *Eun.* 479),[45] but that is rather different. Longus is probably indebted in this matter not to Comedy so much as to moralising literature and to rhetoric: at the conclusion of the *Euboicus* (cf. above pp. 66–7) Dio treats sexual relations with young boys as the ultimate result of urban jadedness (i.e. such affairs have no value beyond a sordid novelty), and a similar contrast between the *mores* of the city and the country is drawn by Libanius in the course of a σύγκρισις ἀγροῦ καὶ πόλεως (8.355 F). This contrast may be traced far back into literary history and it is interesting that Comedy had in fact used these themes: in the *Acharnians* of Aristophanes the countryside is associated with simple and straightforward sexual enjoyment (cf. vv. 263–79), whereas the urban politicians who pursue the war for their own profit are, we feel sure, among the λαικασταί τε καὶ καταπύγονες (v. 79).[46] In the *Casina* of Plautus this situation has been reversed: in that play the old lecher Lysidamus and his bailiff Olympio indulge in a relatively large amount of homosexual by-play and this should be seen as indicative of the fact that their lewd, rustic schemes are offensive to the bourgeois decency of Comedy and are thus bound to fail.⁴⁷ In *D&C*, however, 'villains' do not remain so for long, and Gnathon plays his part honourably at the end; it is also particularly neat that his request to Daphnis at 4.12.1, παρασχεῖν τοιοῦτον οἶον αἱ αἶγες τοῖς τράγοις, repeats what Daphnis and Chloe had already tried without much success (3.14.5).⁴⁸

The relationship with Daphnis at which Gnathon aims is a purely physical one, lacking the educational value which the Greek philosophical tradition sought in such pairings; Daphnis would be merely a 'sex object', an ἐμπαροίνημα (4.18.1, 4.19.5). Homosexuality was frequently attacked by the moralists of the Empire,⁴⁹ and the σύγκρισις of hetero- and homosexual relations was established as a standard theme of Hellenistic and later poetry⁵⁰ and is particularly familiar from the amatory dialogues of Plutarch and Pseudo-Lucian and the discussion of this topic in the novel of Achilles Tatius (2.35-6).⁵¹ It is perhaps not surprising that novels which celebrate heterosexual marriage should treat paederasty and homosexual relations in general in an unfavourable light,⁵² but affairs of this kind in which there is affection on both sides are handled sympathetically by Xenophon of Ephesus (Hippothoos and Cleisthenes) and Achilles (Cleinias and Charicles), although this latter relationship ends unhappily, as also in Achilles' novel does the passion of the sympathetic Menelaus for an anonymous youth (2.34). Longus may also have drawn on the bucolic tradition in his portrayal of Gnathon: in Theocr. *Epigr.* 3 Pan and Priapus intend to rape the sleeping Daphnis and, although Daphnis' rejection of Gnathon based on the lack of homosexual relations in the animal world (4.12.2) uses a common argument (cf. Pl. *Laws* 8.836c, Plut. *Mor.* 990d, [Lucian], *Am.* 22, Straton, *AP* 12.245, Agathias, *AP* 10.68 (= 53 Viansino)), Longus may have picked up a hint from the following exchange between Lacon and Comatas in Theocr. 5:

Λακ. καὶ πόκ' ἐγὼν παρὰ τεῦς τι μαθὼν καλὸν ἢ καὶ ἀκούσας
μέμναμ', ὦ φθονερὸν τὺ καὶ ἀπρεπὲς ἀνδρίον αὕτως;
Κο. ἀνίκ' ἐπύγιζόν τυ, τὺ δ' ἄλγεες· αἱ δὲ χίμαιραι
αἵδε κατεβληχῶντο, καὶ ὁ τράγος αὐτὰς ἐτρύπη. (vv. 39-42)

The behaviour of Theocritus' countrymen here is not only paralleled by the actions of their goats, but also shown up as degraded because the goats behave in a 'normal' heterosexual fashion.[53]

I return now to three of the individual episodes which are elaborated so that they take on a life of their own. I have already noted (above pp. 27–8) that the similarity between the exchange of oaths at 2.39 and Catullus' *Acme and Septimius* points to a common Hellenistic background, and the same is true for other cases also. In 1.25 Daphnis delivers a soliloquy over the sleeping Chloe; this is a situation which is found also in Propertius 1.3 and in epigrams by Philodemus (*AP* 5.123 = *GP* 3212) and Paulus Silentarius (*AP* 5.275). The parallel between 1.25.2, οἷοι καθεύδουσιν ὀφθαλμοί, οἷον δὲ ἀποπνεῖ τὸ στόμα·οὐδὲ τὰ μῆλα τοιοῦτον οὐδὲ αἱ ὄχναι, and a description of the sleeping Ariadne (cf. Prop. 1.3.1–2) at Philostr. *Imag.* 1.15.3, οἷον . . . καὶ ὡς ἡδὺ τὸ ἆσθμα. εἰ δὲ μήλων ἢ βοτρύων ἀπόξει, φιλήσας ἐρεῖς, strongly suggests that Longus is here drawing upon earlier erotic literature.[54] In the poems of Propertius and Paulus the lover takes advantage (or thinks of doing so) of his beloved's slumber, and it is therefore amusing that when Daphnis is placed in the same position he would not know what to do to Chloe even if he felt desire rising in him. In the third book Daphnis appears in another classic position of the Hellenistic lover, outside a locked door, and like many of his literary predecessors he has to endure weather far from suitable for a κῶμος (cf., e.g., Asclepiades, *AP* 5.64 = *HE* 854–9). Unlike his predecessors, however, Daphnis gives up his wait only to discover that he really is very welcome inside the house of his beloved.[55]

A passage in which Longus' debt to the rhetorical tradition is particularly clear is the description of Lamon's garden in 4.2–3. Such an ἔκφρασις κήπου is a common sophistic theme, and Longus here makes use of Homer's description of the garden of Alcinous in *Odyssey* 7, which was the standard poetic model for this type of description.[56] The fact that Longus is working within a well-established tradition does not, of course, necessarily mean that his garden is purely a

product of fantasy. Pierre Grimal[57] has drawn attention to
the oriental character of this garden, and this would be
readily explicable from the geographical position of Lesbos:
the garden would, on this hypothesis, be a mixture of 'literature' and 'life' of a type which may be illustrated from
almost any page of any ancient novel. It is worth noting here
the characteristic restraint of Longus' description, which is
free from over-elaborate artifice. In accordance with the main
themes of his work Longus stresses the *ars/natura* contrast
and the idea of μίμησις,[58] and he avoids the full battery of
rhetoric and wit with which Achilles Tatius assaults his
readers.

Appendix A: Longus and Sappho

I have already discussed one instance where Longus has probably
echoed the poetry of Sappho (above p. 62) and I wish now to examine
in more detail his use of the Lesbian poetess. The subject-matter of
D&C made it almost inevitable that Longus would on occasion exploit
the poetry of Sappho who was regarded throughout antiquity as *the*
poet of love[59] and this may well have been an important factor in the
choice of Lesbos as the setting of the novel. It is, however, not always
easy to distinguish deliberate echoes of Sappho from commonplaces of
erotic literature which may in fact derive from her but were no longer
specifically connected with her. At 1.17.4, χλωρότερον τὸ πρόσωπον
ἦν πόας θερινῆς[60] is a clear echo of Sappho 31.14–15 LP-V, χλωροτέρα
δὲ ποίας| ἔμμι, with the characteristic addition of a specifying adjective
to point up the closeness of Longus' characters to nature (cf. above p.
62 on 1.17.3). It seems likely that Daphnis' account of his symptoms at
1.18.1, ἐκπηδᾶι μου τὸ πνεῦμα, ἐξάλλεται ἡ καρδία, is intended to
recall vv. 5–6 of the same poem, τό μ' ἦ μὰν| καρδίαν ἐν στήθεσιν
ἐπτόαισεν, not only because of this poem's fame and influence,[61] but
also because it would be very much in Longus' manner to use echoes
of the same poem to describe first one and then the other of the
children. This same Sapphic poem may also lie behind Philetas' mem-
ories of young love at 2.7.5, ἤλγουν τὴν ψυχήν, τὴν καρδίαν ἐπαλλόμην,
τὸ σῶμα ἐψυχόμην. Much more doubtful is whether Daphnis' conclusion at 3.14.3 after he has seen the goats rutting, γλυκύ τι ὡς ἔοικέν
ἐστι τὸ ἔργον καὶ νικᾶι τὸ ἔρωτος πικρόν, is intended to echo Sappho
130 LP-V, ἔρος δηὖτέ μ' ὁ λυσιμέλης δόνει,| γλυκύπικρον ἀμάχανον
ὄρπετον. The theme of τὸ γλυκύπικρον ἔρωτος is one of the most
common erotic motifs,[62] and no specific debt to Sappho need be
postulated here. Nevertheless, it may be worth noting that, immediately

THE LITERARY TEXTURE

after quoting γλυκύπικρον from Sappho, Maximus of Tyre (18.9 H) quotes her description of ἔρως as μυθοπλόκος (fr. 188 LP–V) and this reminds us of D&C 2.27.2 where Pan addresses the leader of the Methymnaeans as follows, (the chapter as a whole echoes Hdt. 1.159) ἀπεσπάσατε δὲ βωμῶν παρθένον ἐξ ἧς Ἔρως μῦθον ποιῆσαι θέλει.⁶³ The account at 3.33.4–34 of how Daphnis climbed an apple tree to get the topmost apple for Chloe exploits a famous fragment of Sappho:⁶⁴

μία μηλέα τετρύγητο καὶ οὔτε καρπὸν εἶχεν οὔτε φύλλον · γυμνοὶ
πάντες ἦσαν οἱ κλάδοι · καὶ ἐν μῆλον ἐπέκειτο ἐν αὐτοῖς ἄκροις
ἀκρότατον, μέγα καὶ καλόν, καὶ τῶν πολλῶν τὴν εὐωδίαν ἐνίκα
μόνον. ἔδεισεν ὁ τρυγῶν ἀνελθεῖν καὶ ἠμέλησε καθελεῖν · τάχα
δὲ καὶ ἐφυλάττετο καλὸν μῆλον ἐρωτικῶι ποιμένι.

(D&C 3.33.4)

οἷον τὸ γλυκύμαλον ἐρεύθεται ἄκρωι ἐπ᾽ ὔσδωι
ἄκρον ἐπ᾽ ἀκροτάτωι, λελάθοντο δὲ μαλοδρόπηες·
οὐ μὰν ἐκλελάθοντ᾽, ἀλλ᾽ οὐκ ἐδύναντ᾽ ἐπίκεσθαι.

(Sappho fr. 105a LP–V)

In paraphrasing this fragment of Sappho, Himerius explains that she here compares the bride to an unplucked fruit (9.16 Colonna) and it is plain that this is the way in which Longus has used this conceit. Daphnis has now won the promise of Chloe's hand and in 3.33.1–2 has worked beside her as a husband would; he now offers her an apple, the traditional token of love and marriage,⁶⁵ and the scene is set appropriately in the season of ripeness and fruitfulness (cf. 3.33.3 echoing Hom. Od. 7.114–21 and Theocr. 7.143–6). The apple is not only a gift to Chloe in return for her virginity which she will soon give to Daphnis,⁶⁶ but it is also a symbol of the girl herself: the plucking of the apple indicates the coming 'plucking' of the bride.⁶⁷ The identity of apple and bride gives point to χρόνος δαπανήσηι κείμενον as one of the dangers to which the apple is exposed (3.34.2): here Daphnis uses a gentle form of the lover's traditional warning to the beloved to accept his entreaties now because when she is old no one will want her love. An earlier case where the beloved is compared to a young plant is Ibycus 288:

Εὐρύαλε γλαυκέων Χαρίτων θάλος ⟨   ⟩
καλλικόμων μελέδημα, σὲ μὲν Κύπρις
ἅ τ᾽ ἀγανοβλέφαρος Πει-
θὼ ῥοδέοισιν ἐν ἄνθεσι θρέψαν.

Daphnis' remark to Chloe, τοῦτο τὸ μῆλον ἔφυσαν ὧραι καλαὶ καὶ φυτὸν καλὸν ἔθρεψε πεπαίνοντος ἡλίου καὶ ἐτήρησε τύχη, lends colour to Page's suggestion ⟨Ὡρᾶν⟩ in v. 1 of Ibycus 288 (a supplement which

74

Page based on Hes. *WD* 73–5).[68] Also to be noted is the similarity between Daphnis' speech and the following passage from one of the wedding-songs of Catullus:

ut flos in saeptis secretus nascitur hortis,
ignotus pecori, nullo conuolsus aratro,
quem mulcent aurae, firmat sol, educat imber;
multi illum pueri, multae optauere puellae:
idem cum tenui carptus defloruit ungui,
nulli illum pueri, nullae optauere puellae:
sic uirgo, dum intacta manet, dum cara suis est;
cum castum amisit polluto corpore florem,
nec pueris iucunda manet, nec cara puellis.
Hymen o Hymenaee, Hymen ades o Hymenaee!   (62.39–48)

It is very tempting to believe that Catullus was here thinking of the anonymous verses quoted by Demetrius, *On style* 106:

οἵαν τὰν ὑάκινθον ἐν ὤρεσι ποίμενες ἄνδρες
† πόσσι καταστείβοισι, χάμαι δέ τε πόρφυρον ἄνθος †[69]

Demetrius does not tell us the provenance of these verses nor does he explain them, but in modern times they have been regularly ascribed to Sappho (= fr. 105c LP, 105b V), and if Catullus echoes them in 62.39–47 then it is very likely that he too considered them to be by Sappho.[70] These verses recall one of the dangers to which the apple/Chloe is exposed, ποίμνιον αὐτὸ πατήσηι νεμόμενον (3.34.2), but more striking is the similarity between 3.34.1 (quoted above) and Cat. 62.41 [*flos*] *quem mulcent aurae, firmat sol, educat imber*. The natural conclusion is that there are more lost verses of Sappho behind *D&C* 3.34.1, very likely from the same poem as 105c LP (105b V) or 105a LP–V, if these fragments are themselves not from the one poem, an hypothesis which this chapter of Longus makes probable and which, for other reasons, has been accepted by many modern scholars.[71] Longus thus ends the third book with an intricate and sophisticated mosaic of Homeric, Sapphic and Theocritean elements which can be enjoyed both by those who know his models and (at a different level) by those who do not.

With Sappho's apple Longus has combined two other 'apple-stories'. Daphnis compares his gift to Chloe to the apple which Paris awarded to Aphrodite, a conceit found also in one of the erotic epistles of Philostratus (62 Benner–Fobes), and ἔλαβε γὰρ κρεῖττον καὶ χρυσοῦ μήλου φίλημα (3.34.3) recalls the story of Atalanta and the Golden Apples of the Hesperides. Just like Hippomenes, Daphnis wins by the gift of a golden apple a girl far more valuable than that apple, and certain hints in earlier literature (cf. esp. Cat. 2.11–13) suggest that there is a rich vein of poetic tradition upon which Longus here draws, and it would not be surprising if Sappho herself had somewhere used

75

the myth of Atalanta. In view of the other links between Longus and the Hellenistic poet Philitas (cf. Appendix B below) it is particularly unfortunate that we do not have more than one and a half verses of the passage in which Philitas referred to the story of Atalanta and the apples (Σ Theocr. 2.120 = Philitas fr. 18 Powell). In any event, this myth does appear as an *exemplum* in the song of the lovesick goatherd who has himself brought apples to Amaryllis[72] at Theocr. 3.40-2, and in *Idyll* 29 the ἐραστής offers to imitate Heracles by fetching the golden apples for his beloved; Longus may have had this latter instance in mind as 3.34.2, ἑρπετὸν φαρμάξηι συρόμενον, perhaps recalls 29.12-13, πόησαι καλίαν μίαν ἔνν [Wilamowitz: εἶν codd.] ἔνι δενδρίωι| ὅππυι [Wilamowitz: ὅππηι et ὅπη codd.] μηδὲν ἀπίξεται ἄγριον ὅρπετον, which, as in Longus, is advice from an ἐραστής to his beloved. It may also be, as Ewen Bowie suggests to me, that in 3.34.2 Longus is thinking of the story of Orpheus' wife Eurydice who was killed by a snake; for Daphnis as Orpheus cf. above pp. 30-1.

Appendix B: Longus and Philitas

In this appendix I shall examine the reasons for believing that Longus may have exploited the poetry of Philitas, the poet whom subsequent generations regarded as the 'father of Hellenistic poetry'. Unfortunately, we must approach Philitas largely through possible imitations by later poets; as much of this later poetry is in Latin, it will be useful first to consider the possibility that, where a similarity between a passage of Latin poetry and a passage of *D&C* is observable, Longus (if he was a native speaker of Greek) may have borrowed directly from the Latin passage or from a Greek translation of the Latin.

That Greek writers of the fourth and fifth centuries A.D. paid increasing attention to Latin literature is well known,[73] but similar evidence from the preceding two hundred years is scarce. It is true that Aulus Gellius (19.9.7) represents some learned Athenians as familiar with Republican Latin poetry (i.e. Catullus, Calvus etc.) and that Triphiodorus, whose poem about the fall of Troy seems clearly indebted to Virgil,[74] must be dated to the third or early fourth century (cf. *POxy.* 2946). We know also that already under Claudian the freedman Polybius wrote a paraphrase or translation of the *Aeneid* (cf. Schanz–Hosius II 506). An interesting case is a hexameter poem about the underworld which is preserved on a papyrus of the second or third century A.D. (*P.Bon.* 4) and which shows clear similarities to the sixth book of Virgil's *Aeneid*. In the judgement of the latest editors[75] the poem is post-Virgilian and indebted either to Virgil or to Virgil's source. It is, further, not improbable that Erycius, *AP* 6.96 (= *GP* 2200), Γλαύκων καὶ Κορύδων οἱ ἐν οὔρεσι βουκολέοντες,|

Ἀρκάδες ἀμφότεροι, τὸν κεραὸν δαμάλαν| Πανί κτλ. is influenced by V. *Ecl.* 7.4, *ambo florentes aetatibus, Arcades ambo,* but it cannot be considered certain.[76] In an interesting article[77] Quintino Cataudella pointed to some close verbal similarities between the novel of Chariton and the fourth book of the *Aeneid,* but the cumulative case is not, in my opinion, strong enough to rule out common Greek sources as the explanation. It has, moreover, been argued seriously that Lucian echoes Horace, Ovid and Juvenal,[78] but the sum total of suggested instances remains small. In a rather different category are a few passages where a Latin poetic source is named by a Greek writer: the poet of *AP* 16.151 (of uncertain date) rejects the Virgilian portrayal of Dido, Plutarch paraphrases Hor. *Epist.* 1.6.40-6 (*Lucullus* 39)[79] and the scholiast on Pl. *Phdr.* 244b cites the name of the Cumaean sibyl from Virgil. The conclusion must be, I think, that if Longus was a native Greek speaker who wrote *D&C* at some time in the first three Christian centuries then echoes of Virgil in the work would be remarkable, but would certainly not defy belief, and echoes of any other Latin poet ought not to be ruled out on *a priori* grounds, but we shall demand a very strong case to be made for them.

In 2.3-7 the old countryman Φιλητᾶς instructs Daphnis and Chloe in the nature and power of Eros. His is, however, not simply a lesson in theory, as he has just encountered the god playing in his garden[80] and been reminded of the pangs of love which he himself suffered in his youth. In Philetas we recognise partly the aretaloge of Hellenistic cult[81] and partly the wise *praeceptor amoris* most familiar to us from Roman elegy.[82] In particular we may be reminded of Tibullus 1.8 in which the poet offers amatory advice to Marathus and Pholoe whom he has observed whispering together; both Tibullus and Philetas pass on their experiences to young couples who are already 'in love'.[83] Longus is also indebted in this passage to three pieces of bucolic poetry. The bucolic precedent for a description of Eros he may have found in the poem of Moschus which is known as Ἔρως δραπέτης (*AP* 9.440 = Moschus 1 Gow). Philetas himself is clearly a descendant of the old ploughman who gives wise advice to a young boy who has tried to snare Eros in the following verses by Bion:

ἰξευτὰς ἔτι κῶρος ἐν ἄλσεϊ δενδράεντι
ὄρνεα θηρεύων τὸν ἀπότροπον εἶδεν Ἔρωτα
ἐσδόμενον πύξοιο ποτὶ κλάδον · ὡς δὲ νόησε,
χαίρων ὤνεκα δὴ μέγα φαίνετο τὤρνεον αὐτῶι,
τὼς καλάμως ἅμα πάντας ἐπ' ἀλλάλοισι συνάπτων
τᾶι καὶ τᾶι τὸν Ἔρωτα μετάλμενον ἀμφεδόκευε.
χὠ παῖς, ἀσχαλάων ὅκα οἱ τέλος οὐδὲν ἀπάντη,
τὼς καλάμως ῥίψας ποτ' ἀροτρέα πρέσβυν ἵκανεν
ὅς νιν τάνδε τέχναν ἐδιδάξατο, καὶ λέγεν αὐτῶι

77

THE LITERARY TEXTURE

καί οἱ δεῖξεν Ἔρωτα καθήμενον. αὐτὰρ ὁ πρέσβυς
μειδιάων κίνησε κάρη καὶ ἀμείβετο παῖδα·
'φείδεο τᾶς θήρας, μηδ' ἐς τόδε τᾦρνεον ἔρχευ.
φεῦγε μακράν· κακόν ἐντι τὸ θηρίον. ὄλβιος ἔσσηι
εἰσόκε μή νιν ἕληις· ἢν δ' ἀνέρος ἐς μέτρον ἔλθηις
οὗτος ὁ νῦν φεύγων καὶ ἀπάλμενος αὐτὸς ἀφ' αὐτῶ
ἐλθὼν ἐξαπίνας κεφαλὰν ἔπι σεῖο καθιξεῖ.'   (fr. 13 Gow)

Longus has combined in the character of Philetas both the wise adviser
of Bion's poem and also the ignorant victim who tries to catch the little
hopping bird which is Eros. Finally, the way in which Philetas is introduced at 2.3.1, τερπομένοις δὲ αὐτοῖς ἐφίσταται πρεσβύτης σισύραν
ἐνδεδυμένος, καρβατίνας ὑποδεδεμένος, πήραν ἐξηρτημένος καὶ τὴν
πήραν παλαιάν, recalls the introduction of the mystical goatherd
Lycidas in Theocritus' Thalysia:

ἐκ μὲν γὰρ λασίοιο δασύτριχος εἶχε τράγοιο
κνακὸν δέρμ' ὤμοισι νέας ταμίσοιο ποτόσδον,
ἀμφὶ δέ οἱ στήθεσσι γέρων ἐσφίγγετο πέπλος
ζωστῆρι πλακερῶι, ῥοικὰν δ' ἔχεν ἀγριελαίω
δεξιτερᾶι κορύναν.   (7.15–19)

This likeness stresses the importance of the role which Philetas is to
play; it may (or may not) be significant that in D&C one of Philetas'
sons is called Tityrus, which is the name both of one of the shepherds
in Lycidas' song in Theocritus, Idyll 7 (v. 72) and of the countryman[84]
in Idyll 3 who minds the goats while the nameless goatherd serenades
Amaryllis, which is also the name of the girl whom the Longan Philetas
wooed and won.[85]

Φιλίτας (or Φιλήτας)[86] of Cos is named at Theocr. 7.40 as a poetic
craftsman whose standards 'Simichidas' has not yet reached; this verse
was interpreted in antiquity to mean that Theocritus was a pupil of
Philitas (Vita Theocr. p. 1 Wendel = Test. B Gow), and it is therefore
attractive to believe that Longus has named his old countryman after
the Coan poet, even though Φιλητᾶς is by itself an apt name for a
magister amoris and the etymology of the name is highlighted by
Longus in 2.5.1 and 2.37.3.[87] Longus' Philetas was in his youth a singer
of bucolic love-songs and an excellent συρικτής (2.3.2, 2.5.3, 2.32.3,
2.35.3–4) and, although we have no clear evidence that Philitas of Cos
wrote bucolic poetry,[88] this is at least a not unreasonable interpretation
of Theocr. 7.40 and one that was apparently made in antiquity. It is,
however, one thing to argue that Longus wants us to think of the Coan
poet, but quite another to argue that there are in D&C echoes of
Philitas' poetry or even 'that Longus is (in 2.3–7) harking back to a
Philetan poetic confrontation with the god Eros'.[89] It is also important
to bear in mind just how scarce is evidence for the reading of Philitas'

78

THE LITERARY TEXTURE

poetry in later antiquity; it is true that Propertius names Philitas as a forerunner in erotic and learned poetry (3.1.1, 3.3.52, 3.9.44,⁹⁰ 4.6.3) and that both Ovid and Propertius suggest that his poems were available for reading and imitation (Ovid, *AA* 3.329, *RA* 759-60, Prop. 2.34.31), but it is to be noted how often Philitas, when explicitly mentioned,⁹¹ appears in a standard pair with Callimachus – the only exception from the seven passages listed above is Prop. 3.3.52 where the whole poem is set in a Callimachean frame – and it would be wise to be cautious in using these passages, and others which testify to the fame of his poetry (Ovid, *Tr.* 1.6.1, *EP* 3.1.58), as evidence for the actual reading of his poetry.⁹² Philitas and Callimachus were the canonical pair of Hellenistic elegists to whom later Roman writers looked (cf. Statius, *Silv.* 1.2.252-5, Quint. 10.1.58). A learned commentary preserved on a papyrus of (probably) the second century A.D. (*POxy.* 2260) does, however, cite two verses of Philitas, one of which was already known in the grammatical tradition (fr. 23 Powell), and there is no reason in my view to reject completely the idea that a littérateur of the second century A.D. could have been familiar with the poetry of Philitas. Nevertheless, this is clearly a matter where caution at least is required.

As it is all but certain that Theocritus exploited the poetry of Philitas, echoes of Theocritus in Philetas' speech in Longus may also be echoes of Philitas: the most obvious are 2.5.4 ἡνίκα ἂν αὐτοὺς εἰς ἐν συναγάγω with Theocr. 6.1-2 εἰς ἕνα χῶρον ... συνάγαγον; 2.6.1 with Theocr. 15.120-2 and 29.12-15 (cf. above p. 60); 2.6.2 εἰ δὲ μὴ μάτην ταύτας τὰς πολιὰς ἔφυσα with Theocr. 14.28 μάταν εἰς ἄνδρα γενειῶν and, particularly striking, 2.7.7 ἔρωτος γὰρ οὐδὲν φάρμακον, οὐ πινόμενον, οὐκ ἐσθιόμενον, οὐκ ἐν ᾠδαῖς λαλούμενον, ὅτι μὴ φίλημα καὶ περιβολὴ καὶ συγκατακλιθῆναι γυμνοῖς σώμασι which imitates and varies Theocr. 11.1-3, οὐδὲν ποττὸν ἔρωτα πεφύκει φάρμακον ἄλλο,| Νικία, οὔτ' ἔγχριστον, ἐμὶν δοκεῖ, οὔτ' ἐπίπαστον,| ἢ ταὶ Πιερίδες. We know both from the scholia on these verses and from elsewhere that already in the *Cyclops* dithyramb of Philoxenus the Cyclops cured his love through song (cf. *PMG* 822), and so Theocritus may here allude to both Philoxenus and Philitas.⁹³ That Callimachus also used Polyphemus as the example of someone who cured his love through song (*Epigr.* 46 Pf. = *HE* 1047) may be thought to strengthen the case for believing that Philitas had used this theme.⁹⁴ A further passage which might preserve Philitan material is 2.7.6 in which Philetas tells of his wooing of Amaryllis, ἐκάλουν τὸν Πᾶνα βοηθὸν ὡς καὶ αὐτὸν τῆς Πίτυος ἐρασθέντα· ἐπῄνουν τὴν Ἠχὼ τὸ Ἀμαρυλλίδος ὄνομα μετ' ἐμὲ καλοῦσαν· κατέκλων τὰς σύριγγας ὅτι μοι τὰς μὲν βοῦς ἔθελγον, Ἀμαρυλλίδα δὲ οὐκ ἦγον. The last motif of this passage, which as a whole echoes the themes of the three narratives of metamorphosis included in *D&C* (cf. above pp. 52-7), recalls Prop. 2.13.3-8:

79

hic [sc. Amor] me tam gracilis uetuit contemnere Musas,
   iussit et Ascraeum sic habitare nemus,
non ut Pieriae quercus mea uerba sequantur,
   aut possim Ismaria ducere ualle feras,
sed magis ut nostro stupefiat Cynthia uersu:
   tunc ego sim Inachio notior arte Lino,

and the whole passage in Longus is like Prop. 1.18.19–32 in which
the unhappy lover complains to nature of his sad plight:

uos eritis testes, si quos habet arbor amores,
   fagus et Arcadio pinus amica deo.
a quotiens teneras resonant mea uerba sub umbras,
   scribitur et uestris Cynthia corticibus!
† an tua quod peperit nobis iniuria curas? †
   quae solum tacitis cognita sunt foribus.
omnia consueui timidus perferre superbae
   iussa neque arguto facta dolore queri.
pro quo diuini fontes et frigida rupes
   et datur inculto tramite dura quies;
et quodcumque meae possunt narrare querelae,
   cogor ad argutas dicere solus auis.
sed qualiscumque es resonent mihi 'Cynthia' siluae,
   nec deserta tuo nomine saxa uacent.

It has been realised that Propertius here puts himself in the role of
Acontius from Callimachus' account of the love of Acontius and
Cydippe, as it can be reconstructed from the paraphrase in Aristaenetus
1.10:[95]

δάκρυα μόνον, οὐχ ὕπνον αἱ νύκτες ἐπῆγον τῶι μειρακίωι (cf.
D&C 2.7.4)· κλαίειν γὰρ αἰδούμενος τὴν ἡμέραν τὸ δάκρυον
ἐταμιεύετο ταῖς νυξίν· ἐκτακεὶς δὲ τὰ μέλη καὶ δυσθυμίαις
μαραινόμενος τὴν χροιὰν (cf. D&C 1.18.2) καὶ τὸ βλέμμα δεινῶς
ὠρακιῶν ἐδεδίει τῶι τεκόντι φανῆναι καὶ εἰς ἀγρὸν ἐπὶ πάσηι
προφάσει τὸν πατέρα φεύγων ἐφοίτα. διόπερ οἱ κομψότεροι τῶν
ἡλικωτῶν Λαέρτην αὐτὸν ἐπωνόμαζον, γηπόνον τὸν νεανίσκον
οἰόμενοι γεγονέναι. ἀλλ' Ἀκοντίωι οὐκ ἀμπελῶνος ἔμελεν, οὐ
σκαπάνης, μόνον δὲ φηγοῖς ὑποκαθήμενος ἢ πτελέαις (cf. Theocr.
3.38, D&C 2.5.3) ὠμίλει τάδε· Εἴθε, ὦ δένδρα, καὶ νοῦς ὑμῖν
γένοιτο καὶ φωνή, ὅπως ἂν εἴπητε μόνον· Κυδίππη καλή· ἢ γοῦν
τοσαῦτα κατὰ τῶν φλοιῶν ἐγκεκολαμμένα φέροιτε γράμματα κτλ.

Finally, a further passage which must be considered in this context is
the opening of the first *Eclogue*:

Tityre, tu patulae recubans sub tegmine fagi,
siluestrem tenui Musam meditaris auena;
nos patriae finis et dulcia linquimus arua.
nos patriam fugimus; tu, Tityre, lentus in umbra
formosam resonare doces Amaryllida siluas.

The skein of allusions in this passage of Virgil may be traced through Gallus, Theocritus and Callimachus;[96] the parallels in Longus 2.5.3 and 2.7.6 may perhaps allow the speculation that in *Acontius and Cydippe* Callimachus was in his turn echoing Philitas. I need not emphasise again the uncertainty of this attempt to identify Philitan material in Longus, but the case here seems at least strong enough to warrant consideration.[97]

I turn now to a later section of the second book of *D&C.* I.M.LeM. DuQuesnay[98] has drawn attention to a series of correspondences between Longus 2.32-7 and a passage from the second *Eclogue* which, he suggests, argues for a common source for Virgil and Longus in Philitas:

o tantum libeat mecum tibi sordida rura
atque humilis habitare casas et figere ceruos,
haedorumque gregem uiridi compellere hibisco!
mecum una in siluis imitabere Pana canendo
(Pan primum calamos cera coniungere pluris
instituit, Pan curat ouis ouiumque magistros),
nec te paeniteat calamo triuisse labellum:
haec eadem ut sciret, quid non faciebat Amyntas?
est mihi disparibus septem compacta cicutis
fistula, Damoetas dono mihi quam dedit olim,
et dixit moriens: 'te nunc habet ista secundum';
dixit Damoetas, inuidit stultus Amyntas.   (*Ecl.* 2.28-39)

To vv. 32-3 correspond Longus 2.35.2, εἴκασεν ἄν τις εἶναι ταύτην ἐκείνην ἥν ὁ Πὰν πρῶτον ἐπήξατο and with vv. 32-7 may be compared Longus' account of the creation of the σύριγξ by Pan in 2.34.3, where Theocr. 8.18-19, σύριγγ᾽ ἂν ἐπόησα καλὰν ἔχω ἐννεάφωνον,| λευκὸν κηρὸν ἔχοισαν ἴσον κάτω ἴσον ἄνωθεν, and the similar account at Ach. Tat. 8.6.4 are also to be noted.[99] With v. 31, *mecum una in siluis imitabere Pana canendo*, may be compared 2.37.1 ὁ Δάφνις Πᾶνα ἐμιμεῖτο[100] (although the two passages refer to the imitation of different aspects of Pan), and to vv. 37-8 corresponds Philetas' gift of his σύριγξ to Daphnis at 2.37.3, an act which has roughly the same initiatory function as Lycidas' gift of a staff to Simichidas at Theocr. 7.128-9 and Linus' gift of a σύριγξ to Gallus at *Ecl.* 6.64-73. As DuQuesnay himself noted, however, a better parallel for *Ecl.* 2.37-8 occurs at 1.29.2-3 where the dying Dorcon hands over his σύριγξ to

Chloe. Both Virgil and Longus are clearly indebted for this motif to Theocr. 6.42–3, τόσσ᾽ εἰπὼν τὸν Δάφνιν ὁ Δαμοίτας ἐφίλησε· | χὼ μὲν τῶι σύριγγ᾽, ὁ δὲ τῶι καλὸν αὐλὸν ἔδωκεν, and to Theocr. 1.128–30 where the dying Daphnis gives his pipes to Pan. As well as the elements of the Theocritean Daphnis which we see in Dorcon at this moment,[101] we may also be reminded of Bion's *Lament for Adonis* where the description of Adonis' corpse,

κεῖται καλὸς Ἄδωνις ἐν ὤρεσι μηρὸν ὀδόντι,
λευκῶι λευκὸν ὀδόντι τυπείς, καὶ Κύπριν ἀνίηι
λεπτὸν ἀποψύχων· τὸ δέ οἱ μέλαν εἴβεται αἷμα
χιονέας κατὰ σαρκός, ὑπ᾽ ὀφρύσι δ᾽ ὄμματα ναρκῆι,
καὶ τὸ ῥόδον φεύγει τῶ χείλεος,   (vv. 7–11)

and Aphrodite's request for a last kiss (vv. 42–53) find parallels in the farewell and death of Longus' oxherd.[102] The whole scene in Longus reminds us of passages from earlier poetry in which a dying man issues instructions about his burial,[103] and such emotional scenes fit easily into the simple stories of 'the Greek novel'; the words of Chaereas at Chariton 5.10.8 as he is about to kill himself are particularly relevant, ἀλλὰ νῦν ἀληθῶς ἀποθανόντος Χαιρέου αἰτοῦμαί σε, Καλλιρόη, χάριν τελευταίαν. ὅταν ἀποθάνω, πρόσελθέ μου τῶι νεκρῶι καὶ εἰ μὲν δύνασαι κλαῦσον· τοῦτο γὰρ ἐμοὶ καὶ ἀθανασίας γενήσεται μεῖζον· εἰπὲ δὲ προσκύψασα τῆι στήληι, κἂν ἀνὴρ καὶ βρέφος ὁρῶσι· Οἴχηι, Χαιρέα, νῦν ἀληθῶς. νῦν ἀπέθανες· ἐγὼ γὰρ ἔμελλον ἐπὶ βασιλέως αἱρεῖσθαι σέ.

In summary, the questions of how strong and important are the correspondences between *D&C* 2.32–7 and *V. Ecl.* 2.31–9 and whether one common source lies behind these two passages seem to me to be ones where disagreement is almost inevitable, and if I have stressed the uncertainty of DuQuesnay's suggestion this should not be interpreted as denying its attractions. We must, unfortunately, wait in the hope that one day the sands of Egypt will be as kind to Philitas as they have been to some of his contemporaries and successors.

The final passage which I wish to consider here is 3.5.4. Cut off from Chloe by the snow and ice of winter, Daphnis sets out to hunt the birds which settle outside her house in the hope that he will see her: τὸ μὲν οὖν μεταξὺ σταδίων ἦν οὐ πλέον δέκα, οὔπω δὲ ἡ χιὼν λελυμένη πολὺν αὐτῶι κάματον παρέσχεν. ἔρωτι δὲ ἄρα πάντα βάσιμα, καὶ πῦρ καὶ ὕδωρ καὶ Σκυθικὴ χιών. In an influential article[104] Jean Hubaux noted the similarity between this passage and Prop. 3.16.11–20,

nec tamen est quisquam, sacros qui laedat amantis:
    Scironis media sic licet ire uia.
quisquis amator erit, Scythicis licet ambulet oris,
    nemo adeo ut noceat barbarus esse uolet.

luna ministrat iter, demonstrant astra salebras,
  ipse Amor accensas percutit ante faces,
saeua canum rabies morsus auertit hiantis:
  huic generi quouis tempore tuta uia est.
sanguine tam paruo quis enim spargatur amantis
  improbus? exclusis fit comes ipsa Venus.

Hubaux suggested that Longus and Propertius have a common ancestor here and he tentatively identified this source as Philitas. There are, however, no good grounds for supposing that both writers are echoing the same passage. That the lover is safe from danger is a theme familiar from both Hellenistic and Roman poetry,[105] and it is often found in connection with the theme of the hardships and dangers that the lover must and is willing to undergo.[106] The best known example on a large scale is Ovid, *Am.* 1.9, and vv. 11–16 of that poem may usefully be compared with Longus:

ibit in aduersos montes duplicataque nimbo
  flumina, congestas exteret ille niues,
nec freta pressurus tumidos causabitur Euros
  aptaque uerrendis sidera quaeret aquis.
quis nisi uel miles uel amans et frigora noctis
  et denso mixtas perferet imbre niues?

The words with which Longus' list of dangers is introduced, ἔρωτι πάντα βάσιμα, seem to have been semi-proverbial, cf. Lucian, *Demosth.* 14 ἔρωτι δὴ πάντα πόρμα. Perhaps the most revealing parallel is a passage from Plutarch's *Dialogue on love* (*Mor.* 760d): ἀνὴρ γὰρ ὑποπλησθεὶς Ἔρωτος οὐδὲν Ἄρεος δεῖται μαχόμενος πολεμίοις, ἀλλὰ τὸν αὐτοῦ θεὸν ἔχων συνότα 'πῦρ καὶ θάλασσαν καὶ πνοὰς τὰς αἰθέρος| περᾶν ἔτοιμος' (*Adesp. Trag.* 408 N²-KS), and to this may be added the following words of Phaedra tό Hippolytus in Seneca's *Phaedra, te uel per ignes, per mare insanum sequar| rupesque et amnes, unda quos torrens rapit* (700–1). The list of dangers (fire, water, etc.) is equally common in non-erotic contexts.[107] These facts seem to me greatly to lessen the likelihood that Propertius and Longus have one specific common ancestor, although it is perhaps not improbable that Longus had in mind the same verses as Plutarch quotes. As for the fact that both writers refer to Scythia, we should note that they employ different aspects of the standard literary view of this region: the harshness of the Scythian winter had been topical ever since Herodotus' account (cf. 4.28–31, 4.50)[108] and, although I have not found another proverbial use of ἡ Σκυθικὴ χιών, such an expression is in no way surprising and is very closely paralleled in Lucian, τοσαύτη ψυχρότης ἐνῆν ὑπὲρ τὴν Κασπιακὴν χίόνα καὶ τὸν κρύσταλλον τὸν Κελτικόν (*hist.scrib.* 19). The 'wastes of Scythia' (ἡ Σκυθῶν ἐρημία) were indeed proverbial for desolation.[109]

CHAPTER FOUR

LANGUAGE AND STYLE

In an earlier chapter (cf. above p. 45) I noted that *D&C* is a prominent example of the tension inherent in bucolic and pastoral literature between the 'simplicity' of the subject-matter and the sophistication of the literary style in which that simplicity is described. In this chapter I shall examine Longus' style in greater detail, but it is to be noted at once that by no means all of the novel is composed in the highly ornate, 'poetic' style with which Longus is most associated. Long sections of narrative are written in a simple, apparently artless style which stands in sharp contrast to the ornate set pieces (cf., e.g., 4.18–26). The result is a pleasing variety which saves the novel from becoming a tedious display of verbal virtuosity.

Like all Hellenistic and later Greek prose with literary pretensions, the language of *D&C* is rhythmical, and in particular it is the *clausulae* of sentences where certain recurrent rhythmical patterns are most marked. An analysis of the whole novel reveals that Longus favours patterns which are familiar from other prose of the later period: –ᴗ–x (17.8%), –ᴗᴗ–ᴗx (9.1%), –ᴗ––ᴗx (9.0%), –––ᴗx (9.0%), –ᴗ––x (7.5%), –ᴗ–ᴗx (6.1%), ––––ᴗx (5.7%).[1] The double trochee, which is almost twice as common in *D&C* at sentence-end as any other *clausula*, was particularly associated with prose of the 'Asianic' school,[2] and the connections between Longus and this school are discussed below (cf. p. 90). In broad terms, the narrative sections of the novel are characterised by the use of a wide variety of *clausulae*, a device which avoids any impression of an insistent, poetic rhythm, whereas the ornate passages have a much more marked *clausula* rhythm: thus, for example, Philetas' speech at 2.3–7 shows the repeated use of a number of easily recognisable patterns such as –ᴗ–x, –ᴗ––x, ––––ᴗ–, –ᴗ–ᴗ–

and ‒◡◡‒◡x and it is clear that this is one of the 'poetic' features of that passage (on which cf. above pp. 77–8). It is doubtful whether there are in *D&C* any instances of unusual *clausulae* used for special effect, but it may be worth suggesting that the rare pattern ‒‒‒‒‒‒ adds a sombre note to the death of Dorcon (1.30.1), an imitative note in the account of the echo (3.21.4), and a note of impressive seriousness at the conclusion of Lamon's speech at 4.19.5, ἐπὶ γυναικῶν ἔργα σπουδάζει.

As I shall be concentrating upon the features which combine to make *D&C* 'prose poetry', the importance of Gunnar Valley's demonstration that at the purely lexical level the language of Longus, far from being rich in poeticisms, is a fairly typical example of literary κοινή ought to be stressed at the outset.[3] The ornate passages achieve their effects through sound, word order, variations in sentence length and occasional quotation, rather than through a consistently precious vocabulary. The narrative passages, on the other hand, are characterised both by a simple purity of diction (καθαρότης)[4] and by the lucid syntax which the ancients designated σαφήνεια or ἀφέλεια[5] and for which Lysias and Xenophon were the classical models. Such a style does not, of course, preclude echoes of classical literature and, with greater or less certainty, we can point to a number of places in these sections where Longus has used a phrase or expression of Thucydides to colour the 'military' part of his narrative.[6] Such learning, however, is never allowed to cloud the lucidity of the narrative, and the obvious appropriateness of this simplicity to a story of naive innocence would have been felt in antiquity even more strongly than it is today. If we turn from style to content, it is noteworthy that Hermogenes illustrates ἔννοιαι ἀφελεῖς ('simple thoughts') by two examples from Theocritus (3.1–2, 1.1), as it is rustics, women and children whom one expects to be ἀφελεῖς (Hermogenes pp. 322–3 R). Here we can see the close link in ancient theory and practice between subject and style.

The most obvious characteristic of the ornate passages – by which I mean such 'set pieces' as the prologue, the descriptions of the seasons, the description of Eros in 2.7, the lament (4.8) and so on – is the concern with symmetry and antithesis in both language and thought.[7] Words and phrases are regularly organised into pairs or more elaborate systems, such as tricola: 2.7.7 may serve as a representative example, ἔρωτος γὰρ οὐδὲν φάρμακον, οὐ πινόμενον, οὐκ ἐσθιόμενον, οὐκ ἐν ὠιδαῖς λαλούμενον, ὅτι μὴ φίλημα καὶ περιβολὴ καὶ συγκατακλιθῆναι γυμνοῖς σώμασι. Both of the tricola in this sentence are 'ascending', that is the syllabic count of each unit is greater than the preceding one, and this is very common, though not universal, in these systems. Longus everywhere shows skill and ingenuity in introducing variety into these verbal systems. Words which are linked by rhyme or assonance may have different syntactic functions, cf. ἐν Λέσβωι θηρῶν ἐν ἄλσει Νυμφῶν (*Proem* 1), ἔπινον, ἔπαιζον, ἐπινίκιον ἑορτὴν ἐμιμοῦντο (2.25.3); rather similar is 2.36.1 where the final element in the series, πίνοντι τοῦ γλεύκους, rhymes with the preceding accusatives but is set off from them by the difference in case. Syntactic variation within matched pairs is a common device, cf. 2.38.2 αἵ τε αἶγες πλησίον τῶν προβάτων ἤιεσαν ὅ τε Δάφνις ἐβάδιζεν ἐγγὺς τῆς Χλόης, 3.9.4 Χλόη μετὰ τῆς μητρός, Δρύας ἅμα Δάφνιδι; this latter example is also noteworthy for the frame Χλόη ... Δάφνιδι around the whole unit,[8] a frame which introduces the more elaborate patterning of the next sentence, Χλόηι μὲν ... ὁ Δάφνις. Δάφνις δὲ ... Χλόης (3.9.5). A simple way to avoid monotony is to vary the syllabic count of matched pairs (cf. 1.1.2 ὄρη θηροτρόφα, πεδία πυροφόρα, γήλοφοι κλημάτων, νομαὶ ποιμνίων, 2.7.1 νεότητι χαίρει καὶ κάλλος διώκει), or indeed simply to vary the rhythm (cf. 1.18.2 ὢ νίκης κακῆς · ὢ νόσου καινῆς). A very simple form of variation occurs at 4.3.1, ἐντεῦθεν εὔοπτον μὲν ἦν τὸ πεδίον, καὶ ἦν ὁρᾶν τοὺς νέμοντας, εὔοπτος δὲ ἡ θάλασσα, καὶ ἑωρῶντο οἱ παραπλέοντες, where εὔοπτον μέν and εὔοπτος δέ are balanced and ἦν ὁρᾶν and ἑωρῶντο show elegant variation. Perhaps the most common device is a changed word order from one half of a pair to the other: this may take the form of a simple chiasmus, cf. 1.18.2 οἷον ἄιδουσιν αἱ ἀηδόνες, ἡ δὲ ἐμὴ σῦριγξ σιωπᾶι· οἷον σκιρτῶσιν οἱ ἔριφοι, κἀγὼ κάθημαι, 3.21.4 ἰδίαι μὲν τῶν κωπῶν τὸν ἦχον, ἰδίαι δὲ τὴν φωνὴν τῶν ναυτῶν, or the result may be more complex as in the following examples: 1.9.2 ἀκούοντες μὲν τῶν ὀρνίθων ἀιδόντων ἦιδον (ABCD) ~ βλέποντες δὲ σκιρτῶντας τοὺς ἄρνας ἥλλοντο κοῦφα (ACBD), 2.4.3 πολλάκις μὲν πράγματα ἔσχον ἐρίφους γαλαθηνοὺς διώκων (ABC) ~ πολλάκις δὲ ἔκαμον μεταθέων μόσχους ἀρτιγεννήτους (ACB). In 3.24.2 we can see a typical mixture of dicola and tricola with considerable internal variation, ὁ μὲν γὰρ ἐνήχετο ἐν τοῖς ποταμοῖς (ABC), ἡ δὲ ἐν ταῖς πηγαῖς ἐλούετο (ACB). ὁ μὲν ἐσύριζεν ἀμιλλώμενος πρὸς τὰς πίτυς (ABDC), ἡ δὲ ἦιδε ταῖς ἀηδόσιν ἐρίζουσα (ABCD). ἐθήρων ἀκρίδας λάλους, ἐλάμβανον τέττιγας ἠχοῦντας (ascending dicolon)· ἄνθη συνέλεγον, δένδρα ἔσειον, ὀπώραν ἤσθιον (tricolon). The last two examples well illustrate the use of synonyms to provide both balance and variety: πράγματα ἔσχον ~ ἔκαμον, διώκων~μεταθέων, ἀμιλλώμενος πρός~ἐρίζουσα with dative, ἐθήρων~ἐλάμβανον, λάλους~ἠχοῦντας. In every such case we must ask whether the words involved are truly synonyms used simply for variety or whether Longus is also being linguistically precise. Thus at 2.35.4, ἐσύριττεν οἷον βοῶν ἀγέληι πρέπον, οἷον αἰπολίωι πρόσφορον, οἷον ποίμναις φίλον, there is variation both in the style of the collective phrases (βοῶν ἀγέληι, αἰπολίωι, ποίμναις) and in the accompanying descriptions (πρέπον, πρόσφορον, φίλον) but whereas no rationale, except alliteration, may be discerned behind the latter, the former reproduces the distinctions made in epic poetry, cf. Hom. Il. 11.678–9 πεντήκοντα βοῶν ἀγέλας, τόσα πώεα οἰῶν,| τόσσα συῶν συβόσια, τόσ᾽ αἰπόλια πλατέ᾽ αἰγῶν, Hes. Theog. 445–6 †βουκολίας τ᾽ ἀγέλας †[9] τε καὶ αἰπόλια πλατέ᾽ αἰγῶν| ποίμναις τ᾽ εἰροπόκων οἰῶν. In 3.24.2 (cited above), ἐθήρων and ἐλάμβανον reveal the relative difficulty of catching grasshoppers and cicadas and, despite 1.26.3 where both ἐπήχησεν and λαλοῦντα refer to a cicada, ἀκρίδας λάλους and τέττιγας ἠχοῦντας preserve a Theocritean distinction, cf. Theocr. 5.34 ἀκρίδες ὧδε λαλεῦντι, 16.94–6 τέττιξ . . . ἀχεῖ ἐν ἀκρεμόνεσσιν and note

7.139 τέττιγες λαλαγεῦντες. At 1.5.3, μίτρα διάχρυσος, ὑποδήματα ἐπίχρυσα, περισκελίδες χρυσαί, the epithets seem to be properly used, although the distinctions between them were probably at times neglected in both the spoken and written language.[10] An interesting case is 1.26.2, ἰδοῦσα . . . τὸν Δάφνιν ἐπὶ τῶι δέει γελῶντα τοῦ φόβου μὲν ἐπαύσατο; although Ammonius defines δέος as πολυχρόνιος κακοῦ ὑπόνοια and φόβος as παραυτίκα πτόησις (de diff. verb. 128 Nickau), the two nouns are used synonymously (cf. LSJ s.vv.) and at Plato, Protagoras 358d-e a distinction between them is a quibble worthy only of Prodicus with his concern for ὀρθοέπεια. Whether Longus here follows Ammonius' prescription is certainly open to doubt — δέος seems more likely to be the παραυτίκα πτόησις which causes Chloe to wake up and Daphnis to laugh — but it is interesting that Longus repeats a distinction ascribed by Plato to a leading member of the 'First Sophistic'. A rather similar instance occurs at 2.7.3, τὰ ἄνθη πάντα Ἔρωτος ἔργα, τὰ φυτὰ πάντα τούτου ποιήματα. Between ἔργα and ποιήματα in this passage little difference can be observed,[11] although ποίημα may carry a mystical and religious connotation not present in ἔργον (cf. Lampe, Patristic lexicon s.v.). At Plato, Charmides 163 b-c Critias, arguing along the lines of a Prodicus (cf. Socrates' response at 163d), distinguishes ποίημα 'a thing made' from ἔργον 'a thing made καλῶς τε καὶ ὠφελίμως'. That Longus does not apparently preserve Critias' distinction is less important than the fact that he has again found a classical authority for his lexical uariatio. At 1.22.2, ὑπὸ γὰρ τοῦ δέρματος πτοηθεῖσαι καὶ ὑπὸ τῶν κυνῶν ὑλακτησάντων ταραχθεῖσαι, the difference between the participles is slight but observable: the former suggests the animals' fright (they thought Dorcon was a wolf), whereas the latter tells us merely that they were upset; at 1.27.2 οὔτε καλαύροπος πληγῆι οὔτε κέντρου προσβολῆι the language is again precise, as πληγή is less appropriate to κέντρον ('goad') than to καλαῦροψ ('staff'); at 2.20.3, καὶ τὰς ἀγέλας ἤλασαν κἀκείνην ἤγαγον, Longus again combines variety with linguistic rectitude: although ἄγειν is used for both animals and humans, ἐλαύνειν is the *uox propria* for 'driving' flocks.[12] My final example is 4.37.2, τόν τε Δρύαντα τῶι Μεγακλεῖ προσήγαγον καὶ τὴν Νάπην τῆι Ῥόδηι συνέστησαν, where προσήγαγον perhaps suggests the social inferiority of Dryas to Megacles (cf. LSJ *s.v.* I 8), whereas συνέστησαν seems to stress the social intimacy which, according to a view widely held among men, women form with each other shortly after their first meeting (cf. LSJ *s.v.* A IV).

Longus' concern for a balanced and pointed vocabulary could be illustrated at much greater length, but I shall confine myself to a few further examples. Words may be linked by sound as well as by function (cf. 1.4.3 γαυλοὶ καὶ αὐλοὶ πλάγιοι, 2.5.2 Κρόνου . . . χρόνου, 2.26.3 σῦριγξ . . . σάλπιγξ),[13] and a particularly neat case is 2.39.6, ὡς κόρη καὶ νέμουσα καὶ νομίζουσα τὰς αἶγας κτλ., in which the participles are etymologically linked but νέμειν is used in its 'pastoral' sense; at 2.3.1, σισύραν ἐνδεδυμένος, καρβατίνας ὑποδεδεμένος we have another example of words matched in both sound and function. There are many gradations of wit in the language of *D&C*: at 4.35.1 πάνυ μέγα καὶ νεανικὸν ἐβόα has a γέρων as subject and this calls attention to the literal meaning of νεανικός which was often used simply to mean 'strong' (cf. 1.29.1); at 3.6.1 there is pleasant wit in the description of Daphnis after he has set up his traps, ἐκαθέζετο τὸ ἐντεῦθεν ὄρνιθας καὶ τὴν Χλόην μεριμνῶν.[14] At 4.17.2, ὑπεκρίνετο τὴν τραγικὴν δυσωδίαν μυσάττεσθαι puns upon τραγικός as 'tragic, pertaining to a tragedy' and 'pertaining to a he-goat', a pun which is signalled by the theatrical term ὑπεκρίνετο.[15] Less subtle perhaps are the pun on αἶγες as 'goats' and 'waves' (a sense found at Artemid. 2.12, Hesych. α 1700 Latte) at 2.15.3, a pun which may reflect badly on the Methymnaeans who make it,[16] and οὐκ αἰσίοις [Scaliger: αἴσιον codd.] ὄρνισιν in the bird-catching scene at 3.6.2 which plays upon αἴσιος ὄρνις in the sense of 'a good omen'. In this list may also be mentioned the play on the moral and pastoral senses of εὐνομία at 1.5.1 and on the moral and musical senses of the same word at

2.35.4; the story of Echo at 3.23.3–4 suggests both meanings of μέλος, 'song' and 'limb',[17] and those critics who see in 2.26.2, δελφῖνες πηδῶντες ἐξ ἁλὸς ταῖς οὐραῖς παίοντες τὰς ναῦς ἔλυον τὰ γομφώματα, a reference to the δελφῖνες which were fish-shaped weights dropped on to enemy ships may be correct.[18]

The ornate style of *D&C* with its balanced phrases, rhymes and assonances must, at least in part, be an attempt to reproduce the characteristics of Greek bucolic poetry in which balance and antithesis are major organising principles.[19] This style is, however, also very reminiscent of the prose of Gorgias and his followers in the late fifth century B.C.: Gorgias' striking use of short rhythmical phrases is illustrated by a few famous passages and was parodied by Plato (cf. further below p. 91). A descendant of the Gorgianic style was practised from the late fourth century B.C. onwards by the school of oratory which is normally designated 'Asianic' and whose founding father was traditionally held to be Hegesias of Magnesia.[20] The links between the Second Sophistic and both Asia and 'Asianic' rhetoric are fundamental to an understanding of the former movement,[21] and it is clear that in the second century A.D. a 'Gorgianic' style of prose was more widely practised than at any time since the classical period of Athens; the two most obvious examples other than Longus in the sphere of fictional writing are Achilles Tatius and Apuleius. It is not unreasonable to suppose that these writers sought to emulate Gorgias' avowed aim of rivalling poetry in its hold on the senses and mind of the hearer; in the case of Longus the prologue has clearly aligned *D&C* with the poetic tradition (cf. above p. 47). Throughout antiquity Gorgianic and 'Asianic' prose was criticised as offending against the general principle that prose should be rhythmical, but not metrical,[22] and that the diction of prose should not be too poetical.[23] Although this latter prescription holds good for *D&C* at the purely lexical level (cf. above p. 85), the overall poetic and musical effect of much of the novel can hardly be denied.

LANGUAGE AND STYLE

An important pre-Longan example of 'prose poetry' which must be noted in this connection is Agathon's encomium of Eros in Plato's *Symposium*: this speech, famous for its elaborate style and Gorgianic concern with balance and antithesis, was much quoted by later rhetoricians (cf. below p. 96) and shares with *D&C* not only stylistic features but also (in part at least) subject-matter. The Platonic Agathon is a perfect model for the mixture of poetry and sophistry that we find in *D&C*, and it can hardly be doubted that Longus was influenced by this speech. It is particularly interesting that Agathon's concluding words dedicate his speech to Eros (*Symp.* 197a), just as *D&C* is an ἀνάθημα to Eros, the Nymphs and Pan (cf. above p. 41). It is further to be noted that in his *Dialogue on love* Plutarch describes the effect of ἡ ἐρωτικὴ μανία in Gorgianic terms, καὶ παρόντες ἐρῶσι καὶ ἀπόντες ποθοῦσι καὶ μεθ᾽ ἡμέραν διώκουσι καὶ νύκτωρ θυραυλοῦσι καὶ νήφοντες καλοῦσι τοὺς καλοὺς καὶ πίνοντες ᾄδουσι (*Mor.* 759b). This may be a parodic imitation of a manner very frequently adopted by prose-writers when describing erotic passion (cf. above pp. 62–3 on Gregory of Corinth).

Longus' concern for symmetry and balance is seen not only in the language of the novel but also in its structure. Throughout the work the two lovers have similar experiences, risk similar dangers and express themselves in similar ways. One episode which deserves a separate analysis here is the beauty contest between Daphnis and Dorcon in which Chloe is both judge and prize (1.16). This must partly be an amusing variation on the similar contest for women for which Lesbos was famed in antiquity,[24] and partly the Longan equivalent of the song contests familiar from Greek bucolic poetry. The actual form of the contest is strongly reminiscent of one of the scenes on the bowl which Theocritus describes in *Idyll* 1:

ἔντοσθεν δὲ γυνά, τι θεῶν δαίδαλμα, τέτυκται,
ἀσκητὰ πέπλωι τε καὶ ἄμπυκι· πὰρ δέ οἱ ἄνδρες
καλὸν ἐθειράζοντες ἀμοιβαδὶς ἄλλοθεν ἄλλος
νεικείουσ᾽ ἐπέεσσι· τὰ δ᾽ οὐ φρενὸς ἅπτεται αὐτᾶς·

91

ἀλλ᾽ ὅκα μὲν τῆνον ποτιδέρκεται ἄνδρα γέλαισα,
ἄλλοκα δ᾽ αὖ ποτὶ τὸν ῥιπτεῖ νόον· οἳ δ᾽ ὑπ᾽ ἔρωτος
δηθὰ κυλοιδιόωντες ἐτώσια μοχθίζοντι.   (1.32-8)

The speeches of Dorcon and Daphnis open with the same pronoun (ἐγώ ... ἐμέ) and the whole chapter is enclosed by a ring formed by the two vocatives, παρθένε ... ὦ παρθένε. Within this frame there is a pleasing mixture of parallelism and chiasmus. Dorcon's arguments may be listed as follows:

A   μείζων εἰμὶ Δάφνιδος
B   cows v. goats
C   Dorcon's beauty
D   Dorcon's birth
E   Daphnis' ugliness
F   Daphnis' smell
G   Daphnis' poverty
H   Daphnis' birth

Daphnis' reply is as follows:

D & H   Daphnis' birth
A & B   Daphnis' goats are bigger than Dorcon's cows; Daphnis cannot do much about A, but the size of his goats is by implication the answer to that charge as well.
F   Daphnis' smell
G   Daphnis' wealth
E   Daphnis' beauty
C   Dorcon's ugliness

Daphnis closes a ring around his own speech by returning at the end to the theme of his birth, thus both beginning and ending his speech where Dorcon ended, which well illustrates Longus' characteristic mixture of parallelism and chiasmus. The same can be seen by noting that CEFG in Dorcon's speech is answered by FGEC: the pairs are reversed but within the pairs the order is once preserved and once changed.

γλυκύτης *in Longus*

It has long been recognised that there is much in both the language and subject-matter of *D&C* which corresponds to the ancient prescription for the style which was described as γλυκύτης, 'sweetness'. We are very fortunate to possess a lengthy discussion of this style by Hermogenes of Tarsus, who was perhaps a contemporary or near-contemporary of Longus, and I give below a translation of the relevant sections of his account. The numbers in the margin refer to the pages of Rabe's edition.

330   The thoughts which are sweet and which exhibit pleasantness (ἡδονή) are in particular all mythical ones, such as 'when Aphrodite was born, the gods held a feast and with them was Poros son of Metis' and the rest of that story from the *Symposium* of Plato (203b), or the story of the cicadas in the *Phaedrus* 'how they were once men before the Muses were born' (259b), or the passage in Demosthenes' speech *Against Aristocrates* 'It is in this court-room only that the gods think it right to be punished by and to punish each other'[25] down to 'that the twelve gods should adjudicate between the Eumenides and Orestes' (Dem. 23.66) . . . First then, as I said, it is mythical ideas which most of all produce sweetness and pleasantness. In second place come tales (διηγήματα) which are like myths, such as the tale of the Trojan War and similar events. Third come tales which have a small mythical element, but are believed more than myths. An example is
331 Herodotus' *History* as a whole; this work contains a few myths – the story of Pan (6.105), of Iacchus (8.65) and perhaps a very few other episodes could be mentioned – but the rest is believed actually to have happened and differs from myth, and so is less sweet than that which is by nature mythical.

    A second kind of thought which exhibits pleasantness and sweetness but which has a quite different effect in varying circumstances – for often it surpasses in pleasantness even mythical tales, while often also falling short even of the third class which I have described – is as follows. Everything which is pleasant to the senses (sight, touch, taste and so on) produces pleasantness also when someone describes it. But some sensual pleasures are shameful and some are not. Ones which are not shameful may be described (ἐκφράζειν) straightforwardly such as beautiful landscapes, splendid vegetation, weaving rivers and so on. These things give pleasure to the sight when we see them and to the ears when someone tells of them; an example is the verses of Sappho, 'the babble of cool water is heard through apple-branches' and 'from the quivering leaves sleep flows down' and in fact the whole of that poem (fr. 2 LP–V). Another example is the following passage from Plato's *Phaedrus*: 'By Hera, this is a pleasant resting-place;

332 for this plane-tree is very tall and spreading etc. etc.' (230b).
Descriptions such as these will produce pleasantness and sweetness. Sensual pleasures which are shameful also produce an
appropriate delight and sweetness when we hear of them, for
whatever each man delights in doing will cause him pleasure also
when it is mentioned: the wanton man will take pleasure in
hearing of wanton actions, the sober man in hearing of sober
actions and in short each man in hearing of his own actions. The
verse ἦ ῥα, καὶ ἀγκὰς ἔμαρπτε Κρόνου παῖς ἦν παράκοιτιν ('and
the son of Kronos caught up his wife in his arms') (*Iliad* 14.346)
exhibits pleasantness in no small degree, and it is a pleasantness
which is sober and does not pass moderate bounds, but the
diction of the verse is far from pleasant: ἔμαρπτε ('caught up') is
not only rough but harsh, and in pronunciation and sound
ἀγκάς ('in his arms') approaches more closely to loftiness (μέγεθος)
than to pleasantness, as you will see if you subtract the element
of meaning from the word. ... But the verse 'beneath them the
good earth sent up fresh grass' (*Iliad* 14.347) and the remainder
of the passage[26] exhibit a greater pleasantness because the thing
described is mythical and naturally sweet to our senses and it was
not shameful to create such thoughts and pleasures. A further
333 example is 'and the dark wave curved over them like a mountain
and hid the god and the mortal woman' (*Odyssey* 11.243–4), and
countless other instances could be found in the poets. In general
all thoughts which concern love are sweet, and these occur in
virtually all of the types of sweetness of thought which I have
mentioned. ...

A further souce of sweetness is to ascribe motivation to
things which by nature lack it, such as 'the countryside and the
trees have no wish to teach me anything, but men in the city do'
334 (Pl. *Phdr.* 230d) ... and when Sappho asks her lyre and it
answers in the poem beginning 'come, noble shell, speak to me'
(fr. 118 LP–V). Herodotus is an even better support for what I
have said. Although his whole work is full of pleasures, he
surpasses himself in pleasantness and sweetness in the story of
what Xerxes did to the Hellespont: 'He ordered those who
lashed the water to say the following barbarous and reckless
things, "O bitter water, your master punishes you in this way
because you wronged him when you had suffered no wrong at his
hands. King Xerxes will cross you, with or without your per-
mission. It is just that no one sacrifices to you as you are a
treacherous[27] and salty stream"' (7.35). In making Xerxes speak
to the water as though it had perception and motivation Herodotus outdoes himself in pleasantness, according to the principle
335 which I have stated. ... The same result is achieved if one ascribes

94

to dumb animals properties peculiar to man, such as when Xenophon says that the dogs frown or smile and believe or disbelieve the tracks (*Cyneg.* 3.5, 4.3, 3.7), and when he says 'the dogs which do not let their clever colleagues go forward but disturb and hinder them are over-confident' (*Cyneg.* 3.7), here 'clever' and 'colleagues' and virtually the whole passage is more suited to humans than to dogs. . . .

336   Sweet diction is the diction appropriate to simplicity (ἀφέλεια) . . . and also poetic diction. [He then notes that in this regard Herodotus is particularly sweet and the Ionian dialect is pleasant because it is poetic.] For the same reason, I think, pleasure is produced when quotations of poetry are woven into the text.

337   . . . In the *Symposium* Plato has rather unsparingly parodied the character of Agathon as a poet and he uses woven-in quotation of this kind. But he does not quote the poems of others, but rather his own, and he apologises in advance so that the composition should not seem entirely free: 'I am led to use verse, to tell how it is he who makes' and he here brings in metre 'Peace among men, windless calm on the sea,| rest for the winds and sleep in troubles' (*Symp.* 197c).[28] Similarly in the *Phaedrus* Plato . . . recites the verse 'as wolves love the lamb, so lovers love a boy' (241d). Not even this, however, did he leave without an apology, but he added an explanatory note (cf. 241e). More-

338 over, you must know that these quotations, whether of one's own or of someone else's poetry, do not produce pure sweetness unless they are interwoven into the text in such a way as to form a single unity with the prose narrative: it is not enough if they are quoted separately like laws and decrees in the text of legal speeches . . .

    To return to my discussion of sweetness of diction: the use of epithets also produces a sweet diction, such as 'Come, o clear-voiced Muses' (Pl. *Phdr.* 237a), and even in poetry which is naturally sweet epithets stand out from their surroundings as being somehow sweeter and as increasing the pleasantness. Thus Stesichorus seems to be particularly pleasant because of his

339 considerable use of epithets. . . .

    The figures which produce sweetness are the same as the figures for simplicity (ἀφέλεια) and purity (καθαρότης) and also the figures for beauty (κάλλος) and for the decorated style (ὁ κεκαλλωπισμένος λόγος). The arrangement of words for the pleasant style is the same as that for the beautiful, that is an arrangement which brings the words close to being metrical: for sweetness must also bring pleasure to the senses through

344 word-order. . . .

    Our account of pleasantness (ἡδονή) and sweetness would also do for charm (ἀβρότης) and the so-called pretty (ὡραῖον) style and anything of that sort. For I consider that all of these are really the same and differ only in name. When we express some thought concerning love or one of the other things peculiar to sweetness and we use the above approach and express our meaning through epithets and poetic words and use *parisosis* of figures appropriate to beauty and use the arrangement I have outlined and make the rhythms dignified and beautiful, the clausulae dignified and simple, then our speech will necessarily be pretty and charming.

The very close link between γλυκύτης and ἡδονή is particularly important, as ἡδύς is the standard epithet in Theocritus for bucolic poetry and stands programmatically at the head of *Idyll* 1 (cf. 1.65, 6.9, 7.89, 8.82, 20.28). Thus in Longus' choice of style we see a blending of rhetorical and poetic traditions.

Hermogenes begins by observing that mythical material is particularly γλυκύς, and when he illustrates this from the story in the *Phaedrus* of how song-crazy men wasted away to become cicadas we cannot but think of the stories of the φάττα, Σῦριγξ and Ἠχώ in *D&C*. It is perhaps significant that Philetas praises Lamon's story of Σῦριγξ as a μῦθον ᾠδῆς γλυκύτερον (2.35.1) but, whether or not this description is of programmatic significance, Longus' stories do share with Plato's μῦθος both the theme of metamorphosis and a musical element and belong to the class of μῦθοι which ancient theoreticians saw as an integral part of γλυκύτης.[29] Hermogenes' other example, the birth of Eros at Pl. *Symp.* 203b, was very popular with later rhetoricians[30] and is obviously not unconnected with the theme of *D&C*. In considering the prologue of the novel, I observed that Longus leaves us in no doubt that we are not to read the work as an account of something that actually happened in the way that, as Hermogenes puts it, most of the events which Herodotus describes are believed to have happened (cf. above p. 47). That Longus was in touch with the same streams of rhetorical teaching as Hermogenes is strongly suggested by the fact that in 2.25–6 he exploits the story of Pan and the Athenians which Hermogenes cites as one of the few true μῦθοι in

Herodotus.[31] Despite the distinctions which Hermogenes draws within Herodotus' *History*, antiquity generally regarded this work as a model of γλυκύτης, particularly because of its 'tall tales' and the Ionic language which was considered poetical in flavour.[32] I have already noted (cf. above pp. 49–50) that the scholiast on Thucydides 1.22.4 defines the scorned ἀγώνισμα of that chapter as ὁ γλυκὺς λόγος and that it was generally believed that the subject of Thucydides' attack was Herodotus.

From the γλυκύτης of myth Hermogenes passes to descriptions of aesthetic pleasures such as the beautiful countryside.[33] The relevance of this section to *D&C* hardly requires elaboration, but the two examples which Hermogenes cites do deserve a moment's attention. The links between Longus and Sappho have already been investigated (above pp. 73–6) and in ancient theory Sappho was selected as a prime example of the γλαφυρός style, which has many links with ἀφέλεια and γλυκύτης:[34] in his discussion of the γλαφυρὸς λόγος 'Demetrius' gives as examples of αἱ ἐν τοῖς πράγμασι χάριτες, νυμφαῖοι κῆποι, ὑμέναιοι, ἔρωτες, ὅλη ἡ Σαπφοῦς ποίησις (*On style* 132). Hermogenes' second example is the famous[35] *locus amoenus* from Plato's *Phaedrus* and this may serve as a reminder that descriptions of nature had become almost *de rigueur* in erotic literature: at the opening of Plutarch's *Dialogue on love* a character is urged to report a conversation περὶ ἔρωτος and is warned, ἄφελε τοῦ λόγου τὸ νῦν ἔχον ἐποποιῶν τε λειμῶνας καὶ σκιὰς καὶ ἄμα κιττοῦ τε καὶ σμιλάκων διαδρομὰς καὶ ὅσ' ἄλλα τοιούτων τόπων ἐπιλαβόμενοι γλίχονται τὸν Πλάτωνος Ἰλισσὸν καὶ τὸν ἄγνον ἐκεῖνον καὶ τὴν ἠρέμα προσάντη πόαν πεφυκυῖαν προθυμότερον ἢ κάλλιον ἐπιγράφεσθαι (*Mor.* 749a), and the links between natural description and human passion in the novel of Achilles Tatius are obvious to all. In Longus the link between human happiness as expressed in ἔρως and natural beauty is at the heart of the work, and so it is important that when Hermogenes comes to differentiate between types of sensual pleasure he uses as illustrations two Homeric episodes in which nature responds to the needs of divine lovers. Here ἔρως enters the analysis for the first time — πᾶσαι αἱ ἐρωτικαὶ ἔννοιαι γλυκεῖαί εἰσιν — and we can see that the links between erotic passion and the movements of nature which Longus exploits in a very individual way were forged by a long tradition of Greek poetry and rhetoric.

It might be tempting to believe that in the episode of the seduction of Daphnis by Lycaenion Longus had in mind (or wants us to think of) the Διὸς ἀπάτη in *Iliad* 14, but there are no clear verbal or thematic echoes which would convert this suggestion into something more certain.

The sections on γλυκύτης as it arises from the 'personification' of animals and inanimate objects and from the use of interwoven quotations of poetry have an obvious relevance to *D&C*.[36] With regard to the former, it is again Longus' restraint that catches our attention: animals are occasionally described in human terms (cf. 1.26.3: the τέττιξ sings ὅμοιον ἱκέτηι χάριν ὁμολογοῦντι τῆς σωτηρίας, 3.13.2: each he-goat guards his wives μή τις αὐτὰς μοιχεύσηι λαθών), but Longus' use of this device is notable for its lack of emphasis. When Dorcon's cattle low sadly after his death we are explicitly told that this was a θρῆνος, ὡς ἐν ποιμέσιν εἰκάζετο καὶ αἰπόλοις (1.31.4), and in describing how the sheep and goats lie listlessly during the absence of Daphnis and Chloe, ἀφανεῖς ὄντας ποθοῦντα, Longus qualifies this phrase by οἶμαι, which is one of the very few authorial interventions of this kind in the narrative (1.32.3).[37] Longus was not, of course, writing to meet a 'prescription' for γλυκύτης and Hermogenes himself recognises that one must look in any writer or orator for a predominant style and not expect other styles to be entirely absent (pp. 220.23–21.5 R). Nevertheless, it is sufficiently plain that Longus expects his readers to be conscious of the scholastic, poetic and rhetorical traditions which lie behind his work, because he has chosen a style entirely suited to his subject, and the way in which his language and phrasing mirror the substance of the thought is one of the greatest attractions of this 'sweet' novel.

NOTES

NOTES

Chapter One

1. Cf. W. Schmid *apud* E. Rohde [1914] 616–18, Perry [1967] 167–8, A. Henrichs' edition of Lollianus (Bonn 1972) 11.
2. Cf. Courtney [1962] 93, Perry [1967] 192, C. A. van Rooy, *Studies in classical satire and related literary theory* (Leiden 1966) 153–5.
3. Cf. Plepelits' translation (Stuttgart 1976) 28–9.
4. Cf. my edition of the fragments of Eubulus (Cambridge 1983) pp. 146–8.
5. The fact that the Florentine manuscript apparently refers to the author as Λόγος gave rise to the theory that Λόγγος is a simple corruption of λόγος and that the author is thus anonymous; the postulated corruption, λόγος to λόγγος, is however hard to credit.
6. Mittelstadt [1964] 6 interprets *IG* XII.2.88 as suggesting that Longus 'was a Roman noble, well-educated in the Greek tradition'. If anything, the national epithets should be reversed.
7. *Römische Studien* (Leipzig–Berlin 1922) 321–3. On *IG* XII.2.88 cf. L. Robert, *REA* 62 (1960) 299–300 [= *Opera minora selecta* II 815–16]. The importance of Dionysus in the novel has, of course, been noted in connection with the priest of *IG* XII.2.249, and K. Tümpel, *Phil.* 48 (1889) 115 n. 31, identified priest and novelist. Merkelbach [1962] 193 notes that the chief priestess of a Dionysiac cult in Rome, which is known from a large inscription now in New York (cf. A. Vogliano and F. Cumont, *AJA*[2] 37 (1933) 215–70), was Pompeia Agrippinilla, wife of the consul of A.D. 150 and a member of a Lesbian family whose connection with Rome went back to Theophanes, the friend and historian of Pompey. It is perhaps worth adding that one of the members of this θίασος was called Φιλητᾶς.
8. Cf. H. J. Mason, 'Longus and the topography of Lesbos' *TAPA* 109 (1979) 149–63, P. Green, 'Longus, Antiphon and the topography of Lesbos' *JHS* 102 (1982) 210–14.
9. Cf. the summary of *D&C* in Nicetas Eugenianus 6.439–50. Psellus, *de operat. daemonum* pp. 48–52 Boissonade mentions Achilles Tatius and Heliodorus, not Achilles and Longus, as Christ–Schmid, *Gr.Litt.*[6] II 824 state. This slip has misled Perry [1967] 350 n. 17.

10. For some words of caution cf. G. Anderson in *Erotica Antiqua* 80.

11. *P.Mil.Vogl.* 124, cf. Vilborg's edition pp. xvi–xvii, Reardon [1971] 334 n. 56. J. Schwartz, 'Achille Tatius et Lucien de Samostate' *AC* 45 (1976) 618-26 argues that Achilles has borrowed from Lucian.

12. The closest parallel is 2.34.3 Πᾶν τοὺς δόνακας ὀργῆι τεμών with Ach. Tat. 8.6.9 τέμνει δὴ τοὺς καλάμους ὑπ' ὀργῆς ὁ Πάν, but this is hardly a striking coincidence.

13. *Pace*, e.g., Garin [1909] 440-2. The parallels between the two novels still suggest a direct relationship to Effe [1982] 65 n. 1.

14. Cf. H. B. Dewing, 'The origin of the accentual prose rhythm in Greek' *AJP* 31 (1910) 312-28. In both Bk 1 and Bk 3 of *D&C* (the two books which I examined) only 35% of *clausulae* could be interpreted as a favoured accentual pattern (i.e. with two or four syllables between the last two stresses). On the rhythms of *D&C* cf. pp. 84-5.

15. For this inflation cf. M. Rostovtzeff, *The social and economic history of the Roman empire*[2] (Oxford 1957) 470-1; the big leap in prices in Egypt (from where all the evidence comes) is not noticeable before the late 260s or the 270s, cf. J. A. Strauss, *ZPE* 11 (1973) 289-95 (slave prices), R. P. Duncan-Jones, *Chiron* 6 (1976) 253-4 (grain prices).

16. Cf. Strauss art. cit.

17. Cf. G. Kennedy in G. W. Bowersock (ed.), *Approaches to the Second Sophistic* (University Park, Pennsylvania 1974) 17-22.

18. I think particularly of the war (πόλεμος ἀκήρυκτος 2.19.3, cf. Scarcella [1970] 107) and the treaty between Methymna and Mytilene which are described in Thucydidean terms: with 3.2.3 cf. Thucyd. 1.2.2 and below p. 126 n. 6.

19. Scarcella [1970] 117.

20. In his appendix to R. Reymer's translation of Heliodorus (Zürich 1950) pp. 334-5 [= *Der griechische Liebesroman* (Zürich 1962) 18-19]. Weinreich's suggestion is taken up by Perry [1967] 351 and elaborated by Mittelstadt [1967].

21. Cf. F. Wirth, *Römische Wandmalerei* (Berlin 1934) 87ff. with Plates 17 and 18 (= Plate 8 in Schönberger's edition of Longus).

22. [1967] 351.

23. Cf. Gow's edition I pp. lxxxii–iii and Effe [1982] 72-5. The most obvious literary memorial other than *D&C* of the interest in Theocritus is Lucian, *DMar.* 1 Macleod, cf. Bompaire [1958] 577.

24. Cf. Mittelstadt [1967].

25. E. W. Leach, 'Sacral-idyllic landscape painting and the poems of Tibullus' First Book' *Latomus* 39 (1980) 47-69.

26. Cf. Cairns [1979] 25, A. W. Bulloch, *PCPS* n.s. 19 (1973) 85-7. Our unfortunately scanty remains of post-Theocritean bucolic suggest a larger erotic element than in Theocritus, cf. W. Arland, *Nachtheokritische Bukolik bis an die Schwelle der lateinischen Bukolik* (diss. Leipzig 1937) 40-51, 78-9, who does not, however, make sufficient allowance for the nature of the evidence.

27. On Longus' simplification of country life see Scarcella [1970] 123, Cresci [1981] 4-8.

28. All references to Alciphron use the numeration of Schepers' second edition (1905), which is also that of the Loeb edition of Benner-Fobes.

29. Cf. the remarks of H. Dörrie in *GGA* 198 (1936) 348.

30. [1894] 46.

31. Alc. 2.8.1 ὅλη δὲ εἰ τοῦ ἄστεος, Πανὶ μὲν καὶ Νύμφαις ἀπεχθομένη, ἃς Ἐπιμηλίδας ἐκάλεις καὶ Δρυάδας καὶ Ναϊάδας ~ Longus 2.39.3 παύεται δὲ [sc. ὁ Πάν] οὐδέποτε Δρυάσιν ἐνοχλῶν καὶ Ἐπιμηλίσι Νύμφαις πράγματα παρέχων. The sexual use of πράγματα παρέχειν occurs also at Alc. 2.35.2.

32. On this character cf. pp. 69-71.

33. On this character cf. p. 67.

34. By going outside the purely rustic epistles, Valley [1926] 91 was able to point to Eudromos in Longus but Dromon at Alc. 3.21.1.

35. There is a useful critique of this aspect of Reich's arguments in C. Sondag, *De nominibus apud Alciphronem propriis* (diss. Bonn 1905) 84.

36. Cf. Dalmeyda [1932] 280 n. 2; G. Shipp, *Modern Greek evidence for the ancient Greek vocabulary* (Sydney 1979) *s.v.*

37. Cf. Bonner [1909] 289.

38. Dalmeyda [1932] 279 suggests that a lost play of Middle or New Comedy, rather than the *Lysistrata*, is the source here, but this seems to me very unlikely. Valley [1926] 74 notes that a statement in Bekker, *Anecdota Graeca* I 25, λέγουσι δὲ τοὺς τοιούτους [sc. τοὺς ἀποσεμνύνοντας ἑαυτούς] καὶ τοξοποιεῖν τὰς ὀφρῦς καὶ ἀνέλκειν καὶ ὠφρυῶσθαι, may suggest that the phrase was not an uncommon one, but this note may also in fact derive from Ar. *Lys.* 8. Moreover, in none of the three literary occurrences of τοξοποιεῖν τὰς ὀφρῦς is the precise meaning ἀποσεμνύνειν ἑαυτόν but rather 'to be angry/worried/fierce'. W. Volkmann, *Studia Alciphronea I: De Alciphrone comoediae imitatore* (diss. Breslau 1886) 10, finds many other echoes of Aristophanes in Alc. 2.16, but the only one which seems probable is δριμὺ βλέπει as an echo of *Frogs* 562, ἔβλεψεν εἴς με δριμύ.

39. Further alleged parallels, which do not seem to me to merit discussion, may be found in Valley [1926] 92-5 and Scarcella [1971] 35. J.-R. Vieillefond, *REG* 92 (1979) 137-8, suggests

that Alc. 1.1.4 is an echo of Longus 3.21.1, but I can see nothing in this.

40. With λαβὼν τὴν σύριγγα ἐπέτρεχον τῆι γλώττηι in Alciphron cf. Longus 1.24.4 ἁρπάζων τὴν σύριγγα τοῖς χείλεσιν αὐτὸς τοὺς καλάμους ἐπέτρεχε.

41. Bonner [1909] 282 argues that Longus here lacks the Orphic element present in Alciphron, but this is to consider the passage in isolation from the rest of the novel; cf. the remarks of Carugno [1955] 155.

42. For Epigonus cf. RE 6.69.

43. For 4.16.4 ~ Alc. 3.3.3 and 3.13.3 cf. pp. 69–70.

44. Cf. D. W. Thompson, A glossary of Greek birds² (Oxford 1936) 175; Bonner [1909] 286.

45. In their note on Hor. C. 1.9.3, R. Nisbet and M. Hubbard make the interesting suggestion that Longus 3.3.2 echoes a lost portion of Alcaeus fr. 338 LP–V. ἐπεπήγει κρύσταλλος may be an echo of Thucyd. 3.23.5.

46. Cf. Bonner [1909] 286.

47. Cf. Bion fr. 2.5–6 Gow, V. Georg. 1.299–304 and Hor. C. 1.4.3 neque iam stabulis gaudet pecus aut arator igni which is particularly close to Longus 3.3.4–3.4.1.

48. Dalmeyda [1932] 284 is very scornful of Alciphron's handiwork, but the naive exaggerations of his characters are a convincing part of the ἠθοποιΐα. νέφος ⟨ὀρνίθων⟩ in Alciphron is derived from Hom. Il. 17.755 (a verse echoed at Longus 2.17.3, cf. p. 61), and cf. also Ar. Birds 295. For the transferred sense of δῆμος in Alc. 2.27.1 cf. LSJ s.v. and F. Conca, RFIC 102 (1974) 421; I wonder whether Alciphron was thinking of Ar. Birds 1583–4 ὄρνιθές τινες | ἐπανιστάμενοι τοῖς δημοτικοῖσιν ὀρνέοις.

49. [1909] 278.

50. Cf. Garin [1909] 454–5 and Carugno [1955] 154.

51. Cf. Garin loc. cit.

52. There are references to olive-trees (2.10.1), laurels and myrtles (2.13.1) and pear-trees (2.27.2, cf. 2.38.2) as well as to the πίτυς. In addition, the following names are formed from tree names: Ἐλατίων (2.4), Δρυαντίδας, Δρυάδης (2.8, 2.39), Κότινος (2.12), Πιτυΐσκος (2.20).

53. Cf. Ar. Frogs 618–19, Herodas 4.78, Men. Periceir. 269, Dover on Ar. Clouds 870. Marsyas is a common illustration in rhetorical literature, cf. Ach. Tat. 3.15.4, Libanius 8.46 F, Philostr. Iun. Imag. 2, Apul. Flor. 3.

54. More recent literature includes G. Carugno, GIF 9 (1956) 347–9; M. Pinto, Vichiana n.s. 2 (1973) 261–8 (with a very good bibliography); J. -R. Vieillefond, REG 92 (1979) 134–6. The most important earlier studies are Reich [1894] 4–25 and K. Meiser,

'Kritische Beiträge zu den Briefen des Rhetors Alkiphron' *SB. Munich* (1904) 191–244.

55. J. Bungarten, *Menanders und Glykeras Brief bei Alkiphron* (diss. Bonn 1967) 201–3, argues that Alciphron should be dated 'möglichst spät' because of his use of Latin literature. For the reading of Latin by educated Greeks cf. pp. 76–7, but it is far from certain that Alciphron does in fact echo Latin literature, despite his obvious use of Latin words in a few comic names (cf. Schmid, *RE* 1.1548). Even for so striking an instance as 4.11.4 ~ Prop. 1.8.33–6 a common Greek source cannot be ruled out; cf. J. C. Yardley, *Phoenix* 34 (1980) 253 on another parallel between Alciphron and Propertius. B. Baldwin, 'The date of Alciphron' *Hermes* 110 (1982) 253–4 argues from 4.19.7 that Alciphron was writing while the famous 'singing statue of Memnon' in Egypt was still 'functioning'. After the end of the second century A.D. we do not find further inscriptions commemorating this wonder, although, as Baldwin points out, there is no evidence for the common statement in modern books that Septimius Severus was connected with or responsible for the statue's demise. Nevertheless, Baldwin's argument is a very weak one. The natural suspicion that Alciphron was not concerned with historical accuracy but merely with listing the canonical 'sights' of Egypt, canonical even though some may have been no longer extant, is strengthened by Himerius *apud* Phot. 373a (6. p. 113 Henry) = XIX Colonna, where the pyramids and the statue of Memnon are described in the present tense as two of the wonders of Egypt, cf. Bungarten op. cit. 124. There is, moreover, no reason to assume that Alciphron knew that the wonderful statue was not yet 'working' in Menander's time.

56. Aelian was a contemporary of the Philostratus who wrote the *Lives of the Sophists* and lived at Rome under Septimius Severus, cf. *Vit.Soph.* pp. 624–5, A. Scholfield's Loeb edition of Aelian, *NA*, I pp. xi–xii.

57. At 2.18.2 Alciphron echoes Ar. *Clouds* 71, where see Dover's note and add J.-R. Vieillefond, 'Note sur le mot φελλεύς', *Mélanges A. M. Desrousseaux* (Paris 1937) 481–4.

58. The sigla are those of the edition of P. L. M. Leone (Milan 1974).

59. *Göttingische Nachrichten* (1898) 158 n. 10, cf. also Bonner [1909] 38–9.

60. Cf. K–G I 105; Schwyzer, *Gr. Gramm.* II 235–6; W. Schmid, *Der Atticismus in seinen Hauptvertretern* (Stuttgart 1887–97) IV 714.

61. Both compounds have been introduced by emendation into E. *Cycl.* 152.

62. Cf. Bonner [1909] 39.

63. P. L. M. Leone, 'Sulle *Epistulae rusticae* di Claudio Eliano' *Annali della facoltà di lettere e filosofia di Università di Macerata* 8 (1975) 43–64, argues for common sources rather than for borrowing by Aelian but produces no new arguments.

Chapter Two

1. Cf. G. Rohde [1937] 35, Geyer [1977] 190.
2. There is a good survey by Jack Lindsay in the appendix to his translation of *D&C* (London 1948). At Lucian, *Kataplous* 5 Hermes delivers three hundred babies to Charon μετὰ τῶν ἐκτιθεμένων, apparently as one day's 'haul' from the whole world. Unfortunately, it is not clear what Lucian imagines the relative number of exposed children to be. On the exposure of children in the second and third centuries cf. H. Grassl, *Sozialökonomische Vorstellungen in der kaiserzeitlichen griechischen Literatur (1–3 Jh. n. Chr.)* (*Historia* Einzelschrift 41, Wiesbaden 1982) 58–64 and, in general, R. Tolles, *Untersuchungen zur Kindesaussetzung bei den Griechen* (diss. Breslau 1941).
3. Cf. Gregory's account of the myth reproduced at Nauck, *TGF*[2] p. 509.
4. For this conceit cf. Crinagoras, *AP* 9.224 (= *GP* 1897–1902) in which Caesar and Zeus are compared because both drank goat's milk.
5. For this motif cf. *h.Dem.* 241, Hes. *Theog.* 492–3 (with M. L. West's note).
6. Cf. Ath. 14.618d; Pausanias 1.22.3; S. *OC* 1600; Roscher's *Lexikon s.v.* Chloe; Nilsson, *Geschichte der gr. Religion*[3] (Munich 1967) I 467.
7. Gow–Page accept Brunck's Δάμων in order to avoid Λᾱμων.
8. Cf. R. Nisbet and M. Hubbard on Hor. *C.* 1.33.14.
9. Cf. Shields [1917] 3–4.
10. Cf. Pape–Benseler, *Wörterbuch der griechischen Eigennamen s.v.*
11. F. Zimmermann, *Münchener Beiträge zur Papyrusforschung und antike Rechtsgeschichte* 19 (1934) 26–7, speaks of a 'mythologische Traktat', A. Körte, *APF* 11 (1935) 282–3, suggests a Μιλησιακὸς λόγος and Merkelbach [1962] 192 n. 3 ascribes the fragment to a 'dionysischer Roman'.
12. Cf. Heiserman [1977] 139.
13. The fundamental work is Chalk [1960], who seems, however, not to have known the excellent discussion in G. Rhode [1937].
14. Cf. R. Nisbet and M. Hubbard's introduction to *C.* 1.4.
15. I follow Catlow in giving the text of V; *uere natus iouis* S: *uer natus orbis* T: *uer renatus orbis est* Lipsius.

16. Cf., e.g., Hermogenes p. 22.15 R.
17. But note 4.2.3 ὁ κόρυμβος ... βότρυν ἐμιμεῖτο, where even plants practise μίμησις.
18. For further instances cf. Chalk [1960] 51 n. 120. This idea is used rather differently in the discussion of hetero- and homosexual love in Achilles Tatius; there the kisses of women are praised for their τέχνη and those of young boys for their artlessness (2.37.7, 2.38.5).
19. Cf., e.g., Pl. *Laws* 3.677b, Max. Tyr. 36.3b H, Ovid, *Fasti* 2.292 *artis ... expers*. In the account of primitive man which Plato puts into the mouth of Protagoras, language was developed through the τέχνη which Prometheus stole from Athena and gave to mankind (*Prt.* 322a).
20. Cf. Plut. *Mor.* 974a (= Democritus fr. 154 D-K), Lucr. 5.1379-87 and Ath. 9.390a citing Alcman 39 and Chamaileon fr. 24 W² where the discovery of μουσική is ascribed to the imitation of the singing of birds. How widespread these ideas are in later rhetorical literature may be illustrated from the following passage of [Lucian], *Amores*: τί δ'; οὐκ ἐν ἀρχῆι μὲν εὐθὺ τοῦ βίου σκέπης δεηθέντες ἄνθρωποι νάκη, θηρία δείραντες, ἠμφιέσαντο; καὶ σπήλυγγας ὁρῶν κρύους καταδύσεις ἐπενόησαν ἢ παλαιῶν ῥιζῶν ἢ φυτῶν αὖα κοιλώματα; τὴν δὲ ἀπὸ τούτων μίμησιν ἐπὶ τὸ κρεῖττον ἀεὶ μετάγοντες ὕφηναν μὲν ἑαυτοῖς χλανίδας, οἴκους δὲ ᾠκίσαντο, καὶ λεληθότως αἱ περὶ ταῦτα τέχναι τὸν χρόνον λαβοῦσαι διδάσκαλον ἀντὶ μὲν λιτῆς ὑφῆς τὸ κάλλιον ἐποίκιλαν, ἀντὶ δὲ εὐτελῶν δωματίων ὑψηλὰ τέρεμνα καὶ λίθων πολυτέλειαν ἐμηχανήσαντο καὶ γυμνὴν τοίχων ἀμορφίαν εὐανθέσι βαφαῖς χρωμάτων κατέγραψαν (*Am.* 34).
21. With Prop. 3.13.35 cf. *D&C* 3.24.2 γυμνοὶ συγκατεκλίθησαν καὶ ἓν δέρμα αἰγὸς ἐπεσύραντο, a bucolic version of the familiar μία χλαῖνα of Theocr. 18.19, Asclepiades, *AP* 5.169 (= *HE* 812-15) etc.
22. Cf. Varro, *RR* 3.1.5; B. Gatz, *Weltalter, goldene Zeit und sinnverwandte Vorstellungen* (Hildesheim 1967) 131-2.
23. The accuracy of Longus' picture of Lesbos has been strongly defended by H. J. Mason, 'Longus and the topography of Lesbos' *TAPA* 109 (1979) 149-63. There are good remarks on this subject by E. L. Bowie in *Erotica Antiqua* 94.
24. Cf. W. Elliger, *Die Darstellung der Landschaft in der gr. Dichtung* (Berlin–New York 1975) 403-16 and Cresci [1981] 5-6.
25. Cf. Gow on Theocr. 1.86, Cresci [1981] 14.
26. In order to obviate this difficulty, Wendel places a lacuna in Σ 7.83 between the mention of Daphnis and the citation of *Syrinx* 3. This seems to me unnecessary, but even if Wendel is correct, the original entry may have run, e.g., καθάπερ ὁ Δάφνις

ἱστορεῖται· ⟨ἐν γὰρ τῶι Σύριγγι περὶ τοῦ Δάφνιδος λέγεται⟩ 'οὐχὶ κτλ.'

27. It is tempting, but would be quite rash, to conclude from Philitas fr. 22 Powell, βουγενέας φάμενος προσεβήσαο μακρὰ μελίσσας, that that poet wrote about the legend of Comatas, cf. von Blumenthal, *RE* 19.2168-9. For Philitas and Longus cf. pp. 76-83.

28. For the problems of ascription which the epigrams of Zonas pose cf. *GP* II pp. 263-4.

29. For Pan and Daphnis cf. Theocr. *Epigr.* 3, Meleager, *AP* 12.128.1-2 (= *HE* 4470-1), 7.535 (= *HE* 4700-05), *Enciclopedia dell'arte antica s.v.* Dafni.

30. For the love oath in the novel cf. Xen. Eph. 1.11.3-6.

31. A. M. Scarcella, 'La donna nel romanzo di Longo Sofista' *GIF* n.s. 3 (1972) 63-84 argues that Lycaenion is not a γυνή but a παλλακή; whatever the truth, ἐπακτόν (3.15.1) stresses that she is an outsider in the rural environment, and one might compare Strepsiades' wife in Ar. *Clouds.*

32. I have found Chimaera (Servius on *Ecl.* 8.68), Echenais (Parthenius, *Erot.Path.* 29), Hedina (Philargyrius on *Ecl.* 5.20), Lyca (ditto), Nais (Theocr. 8.43, 94, Ovid, *AA* 1.732), Pimplea (Servius on *Ecl.* 8.68), Nomia (ditto), Thaleia (*Hypoth.* Theocr. 8, Servius on *Ecl.* 8.68), Xenea (Theocr. 7.73).

33. Cf. Roscher's *Lexikon s.v.* Daphnis 957, Wojaczek [1969] 12.

34. In Alc. 1.11.4 the daughter of a fisherman writes that if she cannot satisfy her desire for the man she loves then she will throw herself into the sea like Sappho; for this form of suicide cf. S. *Phil.* 1001-2. At the back of Longus' mind may also have been Theognis 173-8 in which the poet advises Cyrnus to avoid poverty even at the cost of throwing oneself into the sea from high cliffs; amusingly, Daphnis wants to use the same method to avoid sudden wealth. The fame of Theognis' verses is attested by the large number of testimonia cited in West's edition.

35. In 6.78 Eratosthenes was probably thinking of the legendary Daphnis, cf. δυσέρως in v. 4 (~ Theocr. 1.85), although it is only an assumption that the Daphnis of this epigram is in fact a shepherd.

36. Does ἐμαλοφόρει in v. 4 indicate that this shepherd was a lover? λευκόχρως in v. 1 more probably refers to Daphnis' attractiveness in the eyes of Pan than to a ritual whitening of the skin, as Wojaczek [1969] 17-18 explains it.

37. Cf. K. Schefold, *Pompejanische Malerei* (Basel 1952) Index *s.v.* Orpheus, *Enciclopedia dell' arte antica s.v.* Orfeo.

38. Note also Libanius 8.359.10-14 F ποίας δὲ οὐ γραφῆς τερπνότερον ἰωνιὰ καὶ ῥοδωνιὰ καὶ λειμῶνες καὶ κλάδοι τέττιγας φέροντες, αὐλοὶ δὲ καὶ σύριγγες νομέων εἰς αὖλιν ἐλαυνόντων βοῶν ἀγελὰς καὶ αἰπόλια καὶ ποίμνια ποίων θεάτρων οὐχ ἡδίω;.

39. I should note also that I see no reason when reading Bk 2 of *D&C* to think of the myth told by Sositheos (*TrGF* 99 F 1a-3) of the abduction by pirates of Daphnis' girl, or of the contest between Heracles and Lityerses in the same play when considering *D&C* 1.16. As for the Dionysiac Daphnis of *Eclogue* 5, this seems to be very much a Virgilian creation, cf. I. M. LeM. DuQuesnay, 'Virgil's Fifth Eclogue: the song of Mopsus and the new Daphnis' *PVS* 16 (1976/7) 18–41, and no connection between that poem and *D&C* can be established.

40. Cf. J. Diggle on *E. Phaethon* 99.

41. The fullest discussion of the role of Eros in *D&C* is Christie [1972] *passim*, esp. Chap. 2.

42. *Pace* Cresci [1981] 22, there is no reason to see in 2.5.2 (οὖτοι παῖς ἐγὼ κτλ.) an echo of Moschus, *Europa* 155-6.

43. τὰς ψυχὰς ἀναπτεροῖ at 2.7.1 is probably a memory of the *Phaedrus* of Plato (cf. 249d): a vague knowledge of Eros in the *Phaedrus* was part of the standard learning of any rhetorician, cf. Max. Tyr. 18.7 H, Men. Rhet. 337.7 Sp.–RW, F. Wilhelm, *RhM* 57 (1902) 62-5 (on Achilles Tatius). Similarly, *D&C* 1.22.4, ἤθελόν τι, ἠγνόουν ὅ, τι θέλουσι, looks like an echo of *Phdr.* 255d ἐρᾶι μὲν οὖν, ὅτου δὲ ἀπορεῖ. The *locus amoenus* of the *Phaedrus* was a classic of its genre, cf. Hermogenes 331.22 R, Aristaenetus 1.3, Lucian, *de domo* 4, [id.] *Am.* 18.31; Theocr. 5.33-4 and 47-8 remind one also of this passage and the links between Plato and Theocritus are investigated by C. Murley, 'Plato's *Phaedrus* and Theocritean Pastoral' *TAPA* 71 (1940) 281-95. Cf. also pp. 56-7 on *Phaedrus* 259a-d.

44. This phrase is particularly reminiscent of κρατεῖ . . . στοιχείων in Longus; for the meaning of *elementa* in Apuleius see J. G. Griffiths ad loc.

45. Cf. Jane Harrison, *Prolegomena to the study of Greek religion*[3] (Cambridge 1922) Chap. 12, M. L. West on Hesiod loc. cit.

46. στιλπνὸς ὡς ἄρτι λελουμένος (2.4.1) does perhaps recall Ar. *Birds* 697 where the Orphic Eros is στίλβων νῶτον πτερύγοιν χρυσαῖν (cf. W. K. C. Guthrie, *Orpheus and Greek religion*[2], London 1952, 95). Editors of Aristophanes, however, rightly cite πόθωι στίλβων of Eros at Anacreon 444 (= 125 Gentili) and cf. also Callistr. *Imag.* 3.4, Eunapius, *Vit.Soph.* p. 459 (= V 2.5 Giangrande).

47. For the influence of the *Symposium* on later rhetorical literature cf. Theon II.66.19 Sp., Men. Rhet. 334 Sp.–RW, Max. Tyr. 18.4 H, Aristeides 43.16 K, [Lucian], *Am.* 32, 37. τί δὲ ἀλλήλους ζητοῦμεν; at Longus 2.8.3 looks like a memory of Aristophanes' speech in the *Symposium* (cf. 191a-d).

48. The parallel between Lucr. 1.21, *quae quoniam rerum naturam*

sola gubernas, and v. 8 of the 'Orphic' *Hymn*, μοῦνος γὰρ τούτων
πάντων οἴηκα κρατύνεις, indicates merely that both poets are
using a formulaic and traditional style.

49. Cf. H. Mähler, *ZPE* 23 (1976) 1-20; Anderson [1982] 54-5.
50. According to Molinié, ἐν μύθοις is merely Hirschig's supplement
    and the manuscript presents a *macula* at this point; earlier editors,
    however, print ἐν μύθοις without comment. On the failings of
    Molinié's edition see G. Anderson, *JHS* 101 (1981) 163-4 and
    B. P. Reardon, *REG* 95 (1982) 157-73.
51. Cf. Aphthonius' similar encomium of σοφία (II.39 Sp.).
52. Cf. Norden [1898] II 845, Reardon [1971] 143-9; the topoi
    of these orations are well analysed by J. Amann, *Die Zeusrede
    des Ailios Aristeides* (Stuttgart 1931) 1-23. For the 'πάντα-
    Motiv' of Longus 2.7.3 cf. Amann p. 15.
53. *Aelius Aristide* (Paris 1923) 312.
54. The use of the *Symposium* is noted by Keil and cf. also W.
    Uerschels, *Der Dionysoshymnos des Ailios Aristeides* (diss.
    Bonn 1962) 113-14. The passage I have quoted is well dis-
    cussed by Uerschels (pp. 73-82) who notes that in describing
    Dionysos as πρεσβύτατος ... καὶ νεώτατος Aristeides probably
    remembers the Eros of the *Symposium*.
55. Cf. Theocr. 15.120-2.
56. It is interesting that the 'Orphic' Eros appears in the Πτέρυγες
    of Simias (fr. 24 Powell) which, together with the other *techno-
    paegnia*, often turns up in bucolic manuscripts, cf. Gow's
    Theocritus II p. 552; with Longus 2.7.2 may be compared v. 11
    of Simias' poem, εἶκε δέ μοι γαῖα, θαλάσσας τε μυχοί, χάλκεος
    οὐρανός τε, cf. Christie [1972] 189-91. The playfulness of
    Longus' use of 'Orphism' is much better appreciated by Angelika
    Geyer, *Das Problem des Realitätsbezuges in der dionysischen
    Bildkunst der Kaiserzeit* (Würzburg 1977) 22-3 than by Wojaczek
    [1969] 67-74.
57. Eros continues ἡνίκα ἂν αὐτοὺς εἰς ἓν συναγάγω τὸ ἑωθινόν;
    Longus may here echo Theocr. 6.1-2 Δαμοίτας καὶ Δάφνις ὁ
    βουκόλος εἰς ἕνα χῶρον| τὰν ἀγέλαν ποκ', Ἄρατε, συνάγαγον
    and this may also have influenced his choice of ποιμαίνειν.
58. Cf. Chariton 4.2.3 ὁ δὲ Πολύχαρμος, οἷα δὴ νεανίας ἀνδρικὸς
    τὴν φύσιν καὶ μὴ δουλεύων Ἔρωτι, χαλεπῶι τυράννωι κτλ.
59. As Chalk [1960] 45 n. 91 notes, Longus may also have been
    influenced by the phrase ποιμαίνειν ἔρωτα for which cf. Theocr.
    11.80, *AP* 12.99.2 (= *HE* 3685), *Orph.* fr. 82 Kern.
60. Cf. Roscher's *Lexikon s.v.* Pan 1467-8; R. Herbig, *Pan* (Frank-
    furt 1949) 63-9.
61. For Dionysus and Pan cf. Dodds on E. *Ba.* 302-4 and for Diony-
    sus and Eros, Aristeides 41.12-13 (quoted on p. 35), Dodds on

E. *Ba.* 402-16. In Anacreon 357 (= 14 Gentili) the playmates of Dionysus are Eros, the Nymphs and Aphrodite.

62. Cf. Shields [1917] 56-67. For the sanctuary of Zeus, Hera and Dionysus cf. L. Robert, *REA* 62 (1960) 285-315 (= *Opera minora selecta* II 801-31), and for the oracle of Orpheus on the island cf. pp. 53-4.

63. With 2.26.1 cf. *h.Dion.* 40; 2.26.5 συνετὰ μὲν οὖν πᾶσιν κτλ. looks like a variation on the wise steersman of the hymn (vv. 15-24); the motif of self-propelled ships (2.29.3) recalls *h.Apollo* 418ff. The name of the leader of the Methymnaeans, Βρύαξις, may be explained by βρυάκτης, an epithet of Pan found in a fragment of a Doric hymn cited by Stobaeus (I p. 38 Wachsmuth; cf. Bergk, *PLG* III⁴ p. 681). The well-known sculptor of the fourth century B.C. called Bryaxis was active in the eastern Aegean, but I cannot see why Longus would have commemorated this figure. On the symptoms of 'panic' as Longus describes them cf. Borgeaud [1979] 137-75, esp. 149-50.

64. Cf. Kroll [1924] 30-2.

65. The temple is decorated with the traditional feats and miracles of the god, cf. Hor. *C.* 2.19, Prop. 3.17.21-8.

66. Dionysophanes was the name of an Ephesian of the Persian Wars period (Hdt. 9.84, Paus. 9.2.2) and of two Athenians of the classical period (Kirchner, *Prosopographia Attica* 4304-5); cf. in general E. Sitting, *De Graecorum nominibus theophoris* (Halle 1911) 86-7.

67. For the evidence see C. O. Brink, *CQ* 40 (1946) 19-22 and F. Wehrli, *Die Schule des Aristoteles²* (Basel-Stuttgart 1969) IX 93.

68. Contrast the sensible remarks of Heiserman [1977] 141 with the speculations of Chalk [1960] 42-3.

69. I have not thought it worthwhile to rebut in detail the speculations of Merkelbach which are adequately treated by R. Turcan, 'Le roman "initiatique": à propos d'un livre récent' *RHR* 163 (1963) 149-99, pp. 186-93, Geyer [1977] and Reardon [1971] 396 n. 204. One minor point: Turcan 189 n. 1 repeats Dalmeyda's observation (p. xvi n. 3) that if Longus was from Lesbos or had anything important to say about Dionysus then we might have expected him to mention the Methymnaean cult of Διόνυσος Φαλλήν (cf. Paus. 10.19.2, Shields [1917] 59-60). With the possible exception of swimming cows, however, Longus shows very little interest in curiosities.

70. On these descriptions cf. P. Friedländer, *Johannes von Gaza und Paulus Silentiarius* (Leipzig-Berlin 1912) 1-103; Schissel [1913]; Harlan [1965].

71. For a detailed comparison between Longus and Achilles in this

regard cf. Philippides [1978] 70-5.

72. Perry [1967] 110, cf. 67-8, 148, 326. Perry cites the advice of Theon (II.74 Sp.) that pupils should practise telling μῦθοι 'in the accusative case', i.e. on someone else's authority, or as legend, in imitation of the ancients who did this ἵνα παραμυθήσωνται τὸ δοκεῖν ἀδύνατα λέγειν.

73. Certain recent critics write as if Achilles was unsure how to handle his tale, cf. R. Scholes and R. Kellogg, *The nature of narrative* (New York 1966) 245, Vilborg's commentary pp. 10, 140. For some further links between Achilles and the tradition of the philosophical dialogue cf. D. A. Russell, *Plutarch* (London 1972) 35.

74. For ἐνάργεια in historiography cf. D. A. Russell on [Longinus] 15.1 and R. Nisbet and M. Hubbard on Hor. *C.* 2.1.17, and for the concept in general G. Zanker, 'Enargeia in the ancient criticism of poetry', *RhM* 124 (1981) 297-311.

75. Cf. Harlan [1965] 91-2.

76. σωφροσύνη in this context is misunderstood by Heiserman [1977] 131 as 'dignified seriousness'.

77. This common idea finds its best-known expression at S. *Ant.* 787-90 καί σ᾽ οὔτ᾽ ἀθανάτων φύξιμος οὐδείς, | οὔθ᾽ ἀμερίων σέ γ᾽ [Nauck: ἐπ᾽] ἀνθρώ-|πων, ὁ δ᾽ ἔχων μέμηνεν, but there is no reason to suppose a specific debt to that passage; if Longus had any direct model, then Theocr. 27.20, οὐ φεύγεις τὸν Ἔρωτα, τὸν οὐ φύγε παρθένος ἄλλη, is the most likely.

78. Cf. P. Turner, 'Daphnis and Chloe: an interpretation' *G&R* n.s. 7 (1960) 117-23.

79. For Homer as a painter cf. also Cic. *TD* 5.114, Ath. 5.182a, Max. Tyr. 26.5 H, Dion. Hal. περὶ μιμήσεως fr. 6 (II p. 214 U-R). It is noteworthy that at *Phaedrus* 275d Plato both hints at and avoids the linguistic ambiguity, δεινὸν γάρ που, ὦ Φαῖδρε, τοῦτ᾽ ἔχει γραφή, καὶ ὡς ἀληθῶς ὅμοιον ζωγραφίαι.

80. The forced chiasmus recommends this text, cf. Seiler ad loc. citing Hdt. 2.182.1. The Florentine manuscript reads εἰκόνα γραφήν, and Brunck conjectured εἰκόνα γραπτήν which Dalmeyda adopts.

81. Cf. Lampe, *Patristic lexicon s.v.* ἱστορία C4; Sophocles, *Greek lexicon of the Roman and Byzantine periods s.vv.*

82. Cf. Pind. *Pyth.* 6.7-14, Isocr. *Euag.* 73-4, Hor. *C.* 3.30.

83. For the sort of tourism which Longus has in mind cf. L. Friedländer, *Roman life and manners under the early Empire*[2] (trans. L. A. Magnus, London 1908) I 323-94, esp. 344 on Lesbos and 378-80 on 'artistic' tours, and Shields [1917] xv-xvi.

84. Cf. Plut. *Mor.* 346f, C. O. Brink's edition of the *Ars Poetica* pp. 368-9.

85. Cf. Dion. Hal. περὶ μιμήσεως fr. 6.1 (II pp. 202-3 U-R), Plut. *Mor.* 17f-18b, 243a-b, Philostr. *Imag.* Proem 1. It is a pity that J. M. Blanchard's occasionally stimulating article, 'Daphnis et Chloe: histoire de la mimesis' *QUCC* 20 (1975) 39-62 is largely vitiated by factual error and idle speculation.

86. Cf. E. W. Tayler, *Nature and art in Renaissance literature* (New York-London 1964). Tayler's discussion of *D&C* (pp. 61-71) rather exaggerates Longus' commitment to φύσις *as opposed to* τέχνη. For another view of φύσις and τέχνη in Longus cf. Christie [1972] 212-17.

87. Cf. Hippocr. *de uictu* 1.11-24, Arist. *Phys.* 2.199a15-16 (quoted on p. 20).

88. On this passage see H. Flashar in *Entretiens de la Fondation Hardt* 25 (1979) 92-3, and on μίμησις in general Bompaire [1958] 21-32.

89. For τύχη here cf. Ach. Tat. 3.6.3 ἀδελφαὶ δὲ καὶ τὴν ἄλλην τύχην αἱ γραφαί; Chariton expresses the same idea as Longus by πάθος ἐρωτικόν (1.1.1). For the τύχη~τέχνη jingle cf. Agathon fr. 6 Snell, Aristaenetus 1.13.2, 22.

90. For such philosophical paintings cf. Cebes, *Pinax*, Cic. *de fin.* 2.21 on Cleanthes, Harlan [1965] 52ff., and for purely rhetorical examples of the same procedure cf. Lucian, *Slander, Heracles.* For the allegorical interpretation of literature by the Stoics cf. R. Pfeiffer, *History of classical scholarship* (Oxford 1968) 237-41. It may be convenient here to refer to the discussion of the proem of *D&C* by C. Imbert, 'Stoic logic and Alexandrian poetics' in M. Schofield, M. Burnyeat and J. Barnes (edd.), *Doubt and dogmatism* (Oxford 1980) 182-216. Imbert sees in this passage a reflection of the Stoic theory of φαντασίαι and 'a paradigm for the analytical or discursive interpretation of a presentational sign' (pp. 197-8). This theory was indeed used by the Stoics, as Imbert points out, to explain literary creation, and it is closely connected with the concept of ἐνάργεια which was clearly in Longus' mind (cf. above pp. 40-1, [Longinus] 15.1 with Russell's note), but the notion of μίμησις seems to me much more relevant to *D&C* than is Stoic theory. There is at best only a general similarity between a φαντασία and the painting as Longus' source of inspiration.

91. *Erotica Antiqua* 133. As an illustration Chalk notes that Ἔρωτος ληιστήριον at 1.32.4 'makes allegorization of 1.28-32 certain'; many readers will, however, see there simply an effective use of a familiar topos (cf. Asclepiades, *AP* 12.50.2 (= *HE* 881), Chalk [1960] 41 n. 63). On this point I agree with Anderson [1982] 136 n. 75.

92. For the sources cf. R. Volkmann, *Die Rhetorik der Griechen und*

*Römer*² (Leipzig 1885, 1963) 429-32, H. Lausberg, *Handbuch der literarischen Rhetorik* (Munich 1960) 441-3.

93. The same words (ἐξηγητής, περιηγητής, μηνύειν, ἑρμηνύειν) are used for both obviously allegorical and for non-allegorical paintings, cf. Philostr. *Imag.* Proem 4 and *passim*; D. Ruhnken, *Timaeus* (1789) pp. 109-13 on Pausanias' usage.

94. Cf. Theocr. 7.51 τὸ μελύδριον ἐξεπόνασα with Gow's note.

95. One thinks perhaps of Myrsilus of Methymna, an historian of the third century B.C., cf. *RE* 16.1148-50.

96. νέοι συντιθέμενοι is normally taken to refer to the exchange of pledges in 2.39, but this disrupts the sequence of scenes, which otherwise follows the narrative closely. It may well be that Longus has sacrificed strict sequence on the altar of euphony, but it may also be worth suggesting that συντιθέμενοι here means either 'placed together' to look after the flocks (cf. 1.8) or 'competing/comparing themselves' in which case the reference would be to the contest of Daphnis and Dorcon at 1.16. It might be relevant that one of the scenes on the bowl described in Theocritus' first and programmatic poem is a verbal contest for the affections of a lady who looks on (vv. 32-8), a scene which Longus certainly remembered elsewhere (cf. pp. 91-2).

97. The best introductory account of this subject is the third chapter of Kroll [1924]; cf. also A. Scobie, *Aspects of the ancient romance and its heritage* (Meisenheim am Glan 1969) 9-16.

98. Cf. K. Kerenyi, *Die griechisch-orientalische Romanliteratur in religionsgeschichtlicher Beleuchtung* (Tübingen 1927) 8-19.

99. For σμῆνος λόγων in Achilles cf. Pl. *R.* 5.450b οὐκ ἴστε ὅσον ἑσμὸν λόγων ἐπεγείρετε; with easy virtuosity Achilles has substituted synonyms for ἑσμόν and ἐπεγείρετε and altered the order of the words. For the contrast of μῦθος and λόγος cf. Pl. *Gorg.* 523a, *Prt.* 324d, *Phaedo* 61b (an instance cited by Theon in his discussion of μῦθος, II.73 Sp.) and, for a fuller discussion, *R.* 2.376e-7a. Plato did not of course invent the distinction, cf. Pind. *Ol.* 1.28-9, M. Nøjgaard, *La fable antique* (Copenhagen 1964) I 126-8, J. -P. Vernant, *Myth and society in ancient Greece* (Bristol 1980) 186-207. Among later instances may be noted Dio Chrys. 1.49, Ach. Tat. 1.17.3 and Max. Tyr. 4.7d-8a H.

100. Cf. Plut. *Mor.* 348a, Theon II.72.28 Sp., Nicolaus III.453.19 Sp., and the anonymous rhetorical fragments in *P.Michigan* 6 (cf. J. G. Winter, *TAPA* 53 (1922) 136-41). Theon discusses the distinction between μῦθος and λόγος at II.73.25-30 Sp.

101. Cf. Walsh [1970] 3, J. Tatum, *Apuleius and the Golden Ass* (Cornell 1979) 100-1.

102. Apparently first by Boissonade whose notes are incorporated in

Seiler's commentary.

103. Cf. F. Pfister, 'Isokrates und die spätere Gliederung der narratio' *Hermes* 68 (1933) 457-60; note also Isocr. *ad Nicoclem* 48.

104. Cf. H. G. Strebel, *Wertung und Wirkung des thukydideischen Geschichtswerkes in der gr.-röm. Literatur* (diss. Munich 1935) 20-4.

105. Cf. Norden [1898] I 91-5, T. P. Wiseman, *Clio's cosmetics* (Leicester 1979) Chap. 9.

106. For rhetorical παίγνια in general cf. A. Pease, 'Things without honor' *CP* 21 (1926) 27-42.

107. For these themes cf. A. L. Wheeler, 'Erotic teaching in Roman elegy and the Greek sources I' *CP* 5 (1910) 440-50. Longus' claim is particularly reminiscent of Prop. 2.34.81-2 *non tamen haec ulli uenient ingrata legenti,* | *siue in amore rudis siue peritus erit.*

108. *Eupor.* 2.11, p. 133 Rose; cf. E. Rohde [1914] 242. The romances which Theodorus cites are those of Iamblichus, Philip of Amphipolis (E. Rohde [1914] 372-3, *RE* 19.2349) and the otherwise unknown Herodian.

109. On this τέχνη ἀλυπίας cf. G. Bond on E. *HF* 503-5.

110. For Zeno see Eunapius, *Vit.Soph.* 497 (= XIX Giangrande) and, for the school in general, Schmid-Stählin, *Geschichte der griechischen Literatur* II.2.1095-6.

111. Theophilus, περὶ οὔρων *Proem* 1; the only doubt about the identification is caused by the fact that Magnus seems to have been a common name for doctors (cf. Kroll, *RE* 14.494). For the title ἰατροσοφιστής cf. also the heading in the manuscript to Palladas' epigram on Magnus (*AP* 11.281) and Suda γ 207 *s.v.* Γέσιος.

112. Cf. G. W. Bowersock, *Greek Sophists in the Roman Empire* (Oxford 1969) 66-9.

113. To the discussions of these passages in Chalk [1960], McCulloh [1970] and Heiserman [1977] add M. Philippides, 'The "digressive" *aitia* in Longus' *CW* 74 (1980/1) 193-9.

114. Two earlier passages which might suggest a link between Pan, Pitys and the wind are Theocr. 1.1-3 and, as Borgeaud [1979] 123-4 notes, Nonnus 42.259 where Pitys flees from Pan's advances and is described as ὀρείασι σύνδρομος αὔραις.

115. Cf. Phanocles fr. 1 Powell; Philostr. *Her.* 28 De Lannoy; Lucian, *adu. indoc.* 11 where the shrine is referred to as τὸ Βακχεῖον; Shields [1917] 59.

116. 4.2.2 in fact echoes *Od.* 7.114-16. Alcinous' garden was the rhetorical model *par excellence* for a garden, cf. n. 56 to Chap. 3.

117. Cf. A. R. Littlewood, 'Romantic paradises: the rôle of the garden in the Byzantine romance' *BMGS* 5 (1979) 95-114.

118. Cf. W. E. Forehand, 'Symbolic gardens in Longus' *Daphnis and*

Chloe' Eranos 74 (1976) 103-12; this article is sensitive to the multi-layer effect of the novel, but I find most of its speculations unhelpful.

119. Cf. Heiserman [1977] 136, Philippides [1978] 246.

120. Cf. Chalk [1960] 40 n. 62; the girl's request for metamorphosis also follows a very familiar pattern in such stories.

121. I am aware that this is a rash statement in view of the popularity of metamorphosis as a literary theme (cf. E. Rhode [1914] 97-100, R. Nisbet and M. Hubbard's commentary on Horace, *Odes* II, p. 334); it is particularly unfortunate that we do not know more of the poem entitled Ὀρνιθογονία by Boio or Boios (cf. F. Jacoby, *FGrHist* IIIb Suppl. I. pp. 582-3).

122. There are some good remarks on this titillating scene in Effe [1982] 79-80.

Chapter Three

1. The most complete survey of Longus' debt to earlier literature is Valley [1926] 79-104 and cf. also Schönberger's commentary *passim*. Scarcella [1971] lists many 'parallels' which are not in fact direct borrowings by Longus.

2. Cf., e.g., 4.10.1 ὁ μὲν ἀρτιγένειος, ὁ δὲ Γνάθων (τουτὶ γὰρ ἐκαλεῖτο) τὸν πώγωνα ξυρώμενος πάλαι ~ Theocr. 6.2-3 ἧς δ᾽ ὃ μὲν αὐτῶν| πυρρός, ὃ δ᾽ ἡμιγένειος. The opening of *Idyll* 6 may also be echoed at 2.5.4 (cf. below p. 79) and Valley [1926] 85-6 argues that 1.16 is a further reflection of the same passage of Theocritus. Another possible example is 2.22.3-4 where Daphnis' words of despair, ἔχω γὰρ νέμειν ἔτι οὐδέν. ἐνταῦθα περιμενῶ κείμενος ἢ θάνατον ἢ πόλεμον δεύτερον, resemble the lament of the goatherd at the end of Theocr. 3, οὐκέτ᾽ ἀείδω,| κεισεῦμαι δὲ πεσών, καὶ τοὶ λύκοι ὧδέ μ᾽ ἔδονται.

3. At 1.13.2, εἴκασεν ἄν τις αὐτὸ χρώιζεσθαι τῆι σκιᾶι τῆς κόμης, Schönberger cites Archil. 31 West ἡ δέ οἱ κόμη| ὤμους κατεσκίαζε καὶ μετάφρενα, but cf. also Anacreon 347.1-2 (= 71 Gentili) καὶ κ[όμη]ς ἥ τοι κατ᾽ ἀβρὸν| ἐσκίαζεν αὐχένα, Ovid, *Met.* 13.844-5, R. Nisbet and M. Hubbard on Hor. *C.* 2.5.23; in quoting the fragment of Archilochus, Synesius remarks οὐκοῦν ἅπαντες οἴονταί τε καὶ λέγουσιν αὐτοφυὲς εἶναι σκιάδειον τὴν κόμην.

4. On this incident cf. Borgeaud [1979] 146-7. Whatever the precise nature of Pan's assistance, it was a standard topic of later literature, cf. Lucian, *bis acc.* 9, *Philopseud.* 3, Gow on *Syrinx* 9-10. For this episode as a μῦθος γλυκύς cf. p. 96.

5. On Longus' debt to Homer see Scarcella [1971] and (more briefly) J. -R. Vieillefond, 'Les imitations d'Homère dans *Daphnis*

et Chloé ou l'humanisme de Longus' in *Mélanges offerts à O. Navarre* (Toulouse 1935) 425-32. For Longus and Theocritus see Reich [1894] 56-65, Valley [1926] 80-8, G. Rohde [1937], E. Vaccarello, 'L'eredità della poesia bucolica nel romanzo di Longo' *Il mondo classico* 5 (1935) 307-25, Mittelstadt [1970], Christie [1972] Chap. 4, and Cresci [1981].

6. For the evidence cf. C. Wendel, *Scholia in Theocritum vetera* (Leipzig 1914) pp. 2-3. With 2.33.3 cf. [Bion] 2.1 Gow, where Σικελόν both refers to the Cyclops and means 'pastoral', and V. *Ecl.* 10.50-1 *ibo et Chalcidico quae sunt mihi condita uersu| carmina pastoris Siculi modulabor auena*, where Servius offers as one interpretation '*ibo et Theocritio stilo canam carmina Euphorionis*'. The number of doubtful cases makes it impossible to compile a definitive list of the *Idylls* echoed by Longus, but for what it is worth I have found no probable traces of *Idylls* 2, 9, 13, 17-19, 21, 24-6, 28, 30: for *Idyll* 23 cf. below n. 43. For a survey of the attempts to define Virgil's knowledge of Theocritus cf. S. Posch, *Beobachtungen zur Theokritnachwirkung bei Vergil* (Innsbruck–Munich 1969).

7. At the back of Longus' mind may also have been Moschus 1.16 Gow (of Eros) πτερόεις ὡς ὄρνις ἐφίπταται ἄλλον ἐπ' ἄλλωι. Theocr. 29.13 is also echoed at 3.34.2, cf. p. 76.

8. πλατύς was normally used of herds of goats, cf. Aelian, *NA* 15.3 (in a discussion of tunny) ἄλλοι δὲ [sc. νήχονται] κατ' ἀγέλας, ὥσπερ οὖν τὰ αἰπόλια, πλατείας νομὰς νενεμημένοι: for this etymology cf. Eustath. *in Hom.* p. 257.23.

9. The Odyssean image, κατέπεφνε| δειπνίσσας, ὥς τίς τε κατέκτανε βοῦν ἐπὶ φάτνηι, may also lie behind Dorcon's words at 1.29.1, οἱ γάρ με ἀσεβεῖς ληισταὶ πρὸ τῶν βοῶν μαχόμενον κατέκοψαν ὡς βοῦν, if the text is sound in that place. (Does 1.20.2 suggest κατέκοψαν ὡς ταῦρον?).

10. For Cobet's παρά cf. Valley [1926] 8.

11. Cf. A. Papanikolaou, *Chariton-Studien* (Göttingen 1973) 25.

12. I have considerable sympathy with the motives of those who would excise 1.30.6 from the text, but Reeve notes that the language of this passage is thoroughly Longan. The humour of the passage is defended by Anderson [1982] 42 with n. 20.

13. It is unlikely that Gregory is quoting accurately, as a glance at the apparatus in Lobel–Page or Voigt will confirm.

14. For στόμα κηρίων γλυκύτερον Schönberger cites Theocr. 1.146, but note also Theocr. 20.26-7 and the ultimate origin in Hom. *Il.* 1.249 τοῦ καὶ ἀπὸ γλώσσης μέλιτος γλυκίων ῥέεν αὐδή.

15. In Longus ῥοῖζος is masculine, whereas in Homer it is feminine (some MSS and citations offer the masculine there too). By ῥοίζωι Longus probably understood συριγμῶι, cf. Σ Hom. *Od.*

9.315, Stephanus' *Thesaurus s.v.* ῥοῖζος.

16. Cf. Christie [1972] 66. For 'foreshadowing' in the other ancient novels cf. T. Hägg, *Narrative technique in ancient Greek romances* (Stockholm 1971) 213-44.

17. The sequence in 3.7.3 is suspiciously abrupt (even for Longus), and I tentatively postulate a lacuna before μικροῦ: Chloe would have been introduced in the missing section.

18. Chloe's many suitors (3.25.1) may also be an echo of the young girl's boast at Theocr. 27.23, πολλοί μ' ἐμνώοντο, νόωι δ' ἐμῶι οὖτις ἕαδε, to which the boy (whose name is Daphnis) replies εἰς καὶ ἐγὼ πολλῶν μνηστὴρ τεὸς ἐνθάδ' ἱκάνω (cf. *D&C* 3.26.1 ἕνα τῶν μνωμένων αὐτὸν ἠρίθμει).

19. Cf. J. D. Denniston, *The Greek particles*[2] (Oxford 1954) 10-11.

20. This motif is of course much earlier in origin, cf. Sappho fr. 44 LP-V (the wedding of Hector and Andromache).

21. Cf. R. Heinze, 'Petron und der griechische Roman' *Hermes* 34 (1899) 494-519, Courtney [1962], Walsh [1970] 78-9, Anderson [1982] 65-7; for a bibliography of reactions to Heinze's views and some further (in my view unconvincing) objections to them cf. G. Sandy, *AJP* 90 (1969) 299-300.

22. Cf. Effe [1982] 66-9, Anderson [1982] 41-2.

23. Cf. W. Schmid *apud* E. Rohde [1914] 611.

24. Schissel [1913]; cf. also the same scholar's *Entwicklungsgeschichte des gr. Romans im Altertum* (Halle 1913) 83-94.

25. At the end of Bk 1 the children are together, but our attention is focused upon Daphnis alone; Schissel's system also does less than justice to 2.1-11 (Philetas), 2.12-18 and 3.1-11 which are entirely concerned with Daphnis, and the division between 2.31 and 32 is at best a very weak one. Similar criticisms could be made of the highly elaborate 'antiphonal structure' for the novel which is set out in the third chapter of Philippides [1978].

26. Cf. Mittelstadt [1964] 109-11.

27. On the literary aspects of this speech cf. H. von Armin, *Hermes* 26 (1891) 397-407; id., *Leben und Werke des Dio von Prusa* (Berlin 1898) 493-504; Dorothea Reuter, *Untersuchungen zum Euboikos des Dion von Prusa* (diss. Leipzig 1932); R. Vischer, *Das einfache Leben* (Göttingen 1965) 157-70; Perry [1967] 70-1; G. Anderson, *Studies in Lucian's comic fiction* (Leiden 1976) 94-8; P. Desideri, *Dione di Prusa* (Messina-Florence 1978) 223-8. F. Jouan, 'Les thèmes romanesques dans l'*Euboicos* de Dion Chrysostome' *REG* 90 (1977) 38-46 scratches an already well-known surface, and I am unconvinced by G. Highet, 'The huntsman and the castaway' *GRBS* 14 (1973) 35-40, that Dio took from New Comedy the pattern of urban trial scene combined with rustic marriage.

28. Cf. P. A. Brunt, 'Aspects of the social thought of Dio Chrysostom and of the Stoics' *PCPS* n.s. 19 (1973) 9-34, Geyer [1977] 195.
29. Cf. Libanius 8.261-7, 349-60 F, Philostr. *Vit.Soph.* p. 572 (the Scythians), F. Cairns, 'Horace, *Epode* 2, Tibullus 1.1 and rhetorical praise of the countryside' *Mus.Phil.Lond.* 1 (1975) 79-91. In both Longus (3.8.2) and Dio (7.65) the children of the house wait at table in place of slaves and Reuter (n. 27) 35-6 notes that this is in accord with Cynic notions of αὐτάρκεια; cf. also Tib. 1.5.34.
30. It is clear from V. *Ecl.* 1.19-25 and Calp. Sic. 7 that Dio is drawing upon traditional material in his narrative of a rustic's trip to the city.
31. Cf. Marisa Berti, *SCO* 16 (1967) 353-8. The excellent discussion of 'comedy' in *D&C* by Heiserman [1977] 130-45 does not always distinguish clearly between Comedy as an ancient dramatic genre and comedy in a more modern and looser sense. C. Corbato, 'Da Menandro a Caritone. Studi sulla genesi del romanzo greco e i suoi rapporti con la commedia nuova (I)' *Quaderni Triestini sul teatro antico* 1 (1968) 5-44, offers a general introduction to the problems in this area.
32. Cf. J. W. H. Walden, 'Stage-terms in Heliodorus's *Aethiopica*' *HSCP* 5 (1894) 1-43; E. Rohde [1914] 376-7; Perry [1967] 75.
33. Cf. Satyrus, *Vita Euripidis* 39.vii.8-22 Arrighetti (= *POxy.* 1176 col. vii) βιασμοὺς παρθένων, ὑποβολὰς παιδίων, ἀναγνωρισμοὺς διά τε δακτυλίων καὶ διὰ δεραίων, ταῦτα γάρ ἐστι δήπου τὰ συνέχοντα τὴν νεωτέραν κωμωιδίαν, ἃ πρὸς ἄκρον ἤγαγεν Εὐριπίδης, Proleg. de com. XVIII b.2.9, 3.9 Koster. Daphnis' tokens (listed at 1.2.3 and 4.21.2) recall Men. *Periceir.* 822-3 [ ]ές τε χλ[ανί]διον|χρυσῇ τε μίτρα; the latter item corresponds also to Chloe's μίτρα διάχρυσος and her περισκελίδες are paralleled in this function at Com. Adesp. 240.27 Austin. With the shepherd's initial decision to take the trinkets and leave the baby, a decision which is altered through pity, cf. E. *Ion* 43-9.
34. The name is that of a typical aristocrat, cf. Ar. *Clouds* 46 (with K. J. Dover's note), Lucian, *Timon* 22, *Kataplous* 8. K. Wendel, *De nominibus bucolicis* (Leipzig 1900) *s.v.*, sees the influence of Comedy in this name, but this is not necessary. Ewen Bowie points out, however, that a Megacles of Mytilene was active in Lesbian politics in the seventh century B.C. (Arist. *Pol.* 5.1311b27) and that Alcaeus may have made this name familiar to later writers as that of a Lesbian aristocrat.
35. Although χορηγίαι and τριηραρχίαι were still types of liturgy at Athens and elsewhere in the second and third centuries A.D. (cf. J. Oehler, *RE* 12.1875-8), Megacles is probably using anachronistic language drawn from the classical period to describe

the public services that the wealthy of Mytilene obviously performed (cf. *IG* XII.2 *passim*, Scarcella [1970] 106 n. 6, G. Anderson in *Erotica Antiqua* 170). For the motif of impoverishment caused by λειτουργίαι cf. Xen. *Oec.* 2.6, Antiph. fr. 204.3-8 Kock, Apul. *Met.* 4.9.

36. Cf. U. Reinhardt, *Mythologische Beispiele in der neuen Komödie* (*Menander, Plautus, Terenz*) Teil I (diss. Mainz 1974) 116-19.

37. Both forms occur as the names of ordinary women, cf. *POxy.* 1678, *PGroningen* 10, Preisigke, *Sammelbuch* I 5631, III 6222.

38. Λύκα (Timocles fr. 25 Kock), Λυκαίνη (Lucian, *DMer.* 12) and Λυκαινίς (Antipater, *AP* 11.327 = *GP* 115 and probably Meleager, *AP* 5.187 = *HE* 4294) are all known as the names of hetaerae and cf. Lat. *lupa, lupanar,* etc. According to Juvenal 6.123, Messalina in the brothel called herself *Lycisca* (cf. Servius on V. *Ecl.* 3.18). For Λυκαίνιον as the name of a respectable lady cf. *AP* 7.298 (= *HE* 3864) and Callimachus, *Epigr.* 53 Pf. (= *HE* 1153).

39. J. Yardley, 'Propertius' Lycinna' *TAPA* 104 (1974) 429-34, suggests that the Cynthia-Propertius-Lycinna triangle in 3.15 is derived from Comedy.

40. Cf. also Men. *Phasma* 28-43 (with my remarks in *MH* 37 (1980) 226). For the motif of idle city-dwellers 'getting away from it all' cf. Libanius 8.358 F.

41. Cf. Effe [1982] 82.

42. Plutarch mentions a Γνάθων of Sicily as a gourmand or gourmet (*Mor.* 1128b), but we have no information on this man's status.

43. Longus is perhaps here also thinking of Theocr. 23, a poem of which there are otherwise no echoes in *D&C.*

44. Cf. Bonner [1909] 282-3. The closest Greek parallel to Gelasimus' words is in fact Alciphron 3.3.1 ἀγχόνης μοι δεῖ, καὶ ὄψει με σὺ μετὰ μικρὸν ἐν βρόχωι τὸν τράχηλον ἔχοντα. Villoison's certain correction at 4.16.4 makes Gnathon swear by his patron Astylus, and this conceit is probably also comic in origin, cf. Lucian, *Kataplous* 11 where the tyrant Megapenthes says of his courtiers ὅλως ὅρκος αὐτοῖς ἦν ἐγώ.

45. Ed. Fraenkel, *Elementi Plautini in Plauto* (Florence 1960) 249 and L. Schaaf, *Der Miles Gloriosus des Plautus und sein griechisches Original* (Munich 1977) 314 are inclined to see *MG* 1111-13 as a Plautine joke added to the Greek original. At Plaut. *Pseud.* 1180-1 in a passage of prolonged abuse, a soldier's batman is accused of homosexual relations with his boss.

46. Cf. J. Henderson, *The maculate muse* (New Haven-London 1975) 58-9.

47. Whether Diphilus or Plautus is mainly responsible for the homosexual element in the play, a problem discussed by Jane Cody,

Hermes 104 (1976) 453–76, is not relevant here.

48. Cf. Fronto, *Epist.* p. 238.8–11 van den Hout (an imitation of the non-lover's speech in Pl. *Phdr.*), εἰ γοῦν ἐπιτρέψειε ⟨σ⟩αυτὸν τῶι ἐραστῆι χρῆσθαι ὅπου καὶ ὁπότε βούλοιτο, οὔτ᾽ ἂν καιρὸν περιμείνας ἐπιτήδειον οὔτε τόπον οὔτε σχολὴν οὔτε ἐρημίαν, ἀλλὰ θηρίου δίκην ὑπὸ λύττης εὐθὺς ἴοιτο ἂν καὶ βαίνειν προθυμοῖτο μηδὲν αἰδούμενος.

49. Cf. Musonius Rufus fr. 12 Hense with the remarks of A. van Geytenbeek, *Musonius Rufus and Greek diatribe* (Assen 1963) 73–4.

50. Cf. Meleager, *AP* 5.208 (= *HE* 4046); Eratosthenes, *AP* 5.277; Agathias, *AP* 5.278 (= 52 Viansino); Rufinus, *AP* 5.19 (= 6 Page); Prop. 2.4.17–18; Ovid, *AA* 2.683–4.

51. Cf. F. Wilhelm, 'Zu Achilles Tatius' *RhM* 57 (1902) 55–75.

52. Observe Callirhoe's angry reply when Chaireas has impugned her honour at Chariton 1.3.6, οὐδεὶς ἐπὶ τὴν πατρώιαν οἰκίαν ἐκώμασεν . . . τὰ δὲ σὰ πρόθυρα συνήθη τυχόν ἐστι τοῖς κώμοις, καὶ τὸ γεγαμηκέναι σε λυπεῖ τοὺς ἐραστάς.

53. Cf. also Cresci [1981] 15–16 for a different view of Longus' use of this passage of Theocritus.

54. For the Ariadne comparison in the novel cf. Chariton 1.6.2.

55. I have considered whether the description of the foliage outside Dryas' house at 3.5.1 is a Longan version of the ivy and fern outside Amaryllis' cave in Theocr. 3, and this suggestion has now been made by Cresci [1981] 8. The reminiscence seems to me possible, but not certain.

56. For ἐκφράσεις κήπου cf. Libanius 8.485–6 F, Ach. Tat. 1.15, Apul. *Met.* 2.4, Aelian, *VH* 3.1 (Tempe), [Lucian], *Am.* 12; for the influence of *Odyssey* 7 cf. Libanius loc. cit., Syrianus, *in Hermog.* 77.3 R, Aristaenetus 1.3.7.

57. *Revue Archéologique*[6] 49 (1957) 211–14, but note also the observation of E. L. Bowie in *Erotica Antiqua* 93 '[the παράδεισος] could be . . . simply an orchard seen through romanticising eyes'.

58. This was a standard theme in such ἐκφράσεις, cf. Ovid. *Met.* 3.158–9 *simulauerat artem| ingenio natura suo*, Aelian, *VH* 3.1.23–4 Dilts, Libanius 8.486.1–2 F and Apul. *Met.* 2.4 (where the garden really is 'a work of art'). Note also Synesius, *Epist.* 114 Hercher ποικίλαι δὲ καὶ ὀρνίθων ὠιδαὶ καὶ ἀνθέων χρόαι καὶ λειμῶνος θάμνοι, τὰ μὲν γεωργίας ἔργα, τὰ δὲ φύσεως δῶρα (cf. *D&C* 2.12.2), πάντα εὐώδη, γῆς ὑγιαινούσης χυμοί· τὸ δὲ τῶν Νυμφῶν ἄντρον οὐκ ἐπαινέσομαι. Θεοκρίτου γὰρ δεῖ.

59. For Sappho's reputation and *Nachleben* cf. H. Dörrie, *P. Ovidius Naso: Der Brief der Sappho an Phaon* (Munich 1975) 9–49 and R. Nisbet and M. Hubbard on Hor. *C.* 2.13.25.

60. πόας θερινῆς Courier: χλόας καιρινῆς F: χλόης θερινῆς F^ssᵃ.
    Chloe's silence which is described in the same chapter is a lasting
    condition unlike the sudden attack of speechlessness which
    Sappho suffers in fr. 31 LP-V and which is imitated at Theocr.
    2.108. ἠμέλητο καὶ ἡ ἀγέλη in Longus is a bucolic example of
    erotic ἀργία which recalls the lovesick Cyclops of Theocr. 11
    (cf. vv. 12-13, 73-4).
61. Cf. Voigt's edition pp. 58-9; R. Stark, 'Sapphoreminiszenzen'
    Hermes 85 (1957) 325-35.
62. Cf. Voigt on Sappho 130.2. For a rhetorical example cf. Libanius
    8.541 F (an ἔκφρασις κάλλους) τὸ μὲν κάλλος γλυκύ, ἡ δὲ τρῶσις
    πικρά. καί πως γλυκύτερον ἦν τὸ λυπεῖν.
63. Cf. Prop. 1.15.23-4, Apul. *Met.* 2.12 (a Chaldaean prophesied
    to Lucius) *nunc ... gloriam satis floridam, nunc historiam
    magnam et incredundam fabulam et libros me futurum.*
64. On this incident cf. Mittelstadt [1970] 225-6. For the theory of
    μίμησις and παράφρασις which lies behind Longus' reworking of
    Sappho here cf. Theon II.59-65 Sp.; Kroll, *RE* Suppl. 7.1113-
    16; Bompaire [1958] 382-404; G. Giangrande, *Eranos* 60
    (1962) 152-9; D. A. Russell, 'De imitatione' in D. West and A.
    Woodman (edd.), *Creative imitation and Latin literature* (Cam-
    bridge 1979) 1-16 and T. Gelzer, *Entretiens de la Fondation
    Hardt* 25 (1979) 33-7.
65. Cf. A. R. Littlewood, 'The symbolism of the apple in Greek and
    Roman literature' *HSCP* 72 (1967) 147-81.
66. Cf. *AP* 5.79 (= Plato, *Epigr.* 4 Page) τῶι μήλωι βάλλω σε· σὺ
    δ', εἰ μὲν ἑκοῦσα φιλεῖς με,│ δεξαμένη τῆς σῆς παρθενίης
    μετάδος κτλ.
67. For τρυγᾶν cf. Ar. *Peace* 1339-40 (omitted in Platnauer's
    edition), Meleager, *AP* 12.256.1 (= *HE* 4408), Ach. Tat. 1.8.9,
    Aelian, *Epist.* 1.
68. For the Horai cf. Headlam on Hds. 7.94-5, Gow on Theocr.
    1.150 and Roscher's *Lexikon s.v.* (esp. 2720-1 on the association
    of the Horai with Helios and the epithet καλαί). The end of
    3.34.1 perhaps also recalls Cat. 61.21-5, *floridis uelut enitens│
    myrtus Asia ramulis│ quos Hamadryades deae│ ludicrum sibi
    roscido│ nutriunt umore,* where Sapphic influence has been
    suspected, cf. P. Fedeli, *Il carme 61 di Catullo* (Fribourg 1972)
    35.
69. ἵνα πέσηι χαμαί in 3.34.2 lends colour to χάμαι 'πέτε which
    Lobel-Page suggest in this verse.
70. Cf. Ed. Fraenkel, *JRS* 45 (1955) 5 (= *Kleine Beiträge* II 94).
71. For the bibliography cf. Voigt ad loc.
72. Cf. V. *Ecl.* 3.70-1 *puero siluestri ex arbore lecta│ aurea mala
    decem misi: cras altera mittam,* which combines Theocr. 3.10-11

with 5.97.

73. Cf. E. A. Fisher, 'Greek translations of Latin literature in the fourth century A.D.' *YCS* 27 (1982) 173–215; V. Reichmann, *Römische Literatur in griechischer Übersetzung (Phil.* Suppl. 34.3, 1943) 9–16; J. Diggle, *Euripides: Phaethon* (Cambridge 1970) 180–204; A. Cameron, *Historia* 14 (1965) 494–6; id., *Claudian: poetry and propaganda at the court of Honorius* (Oxford 1970) 19–21.

74. Cf. the bibliography at Cameron, *Claudian* (preceding note) 20 n. 5.

75. Cf. H. Lloyd-Jones and P. J. Parsons, 'Iterum de "Catabasi Orphica"' in *Kyklos: Festschrift Rudolf Keydell* (Berlin–New York 1978) 88–100.

76. Virgilian influence is rejected by Gow–Page. *POxy.* 2886 (b) 7ff. (a reference which I owe to the kindness of Peter Parsons) contains a commentary on verses (probably hexameters) which were clearly similar to V. *Aen.* 4.261–3; Lobel dated the papyrus to the second century A.D. but the poem was very likely pre-Virgilian.

77. 'Riflessi Virgiliani nel romanzo di Caritone' *Athenaeum* n.s. 5 (1927) 302–12.

78. For Lucian and Horace cf. J. Hall, *Lucian's satire* (New York 1981) 110–21; for Lucian and Juvenal cf. J. Mesk, 'Lucians Nigrinus und Juvenal' *WS* 34 (1912) 373–82 and 35 (1913) 1–33 and Bompaire [1958] 504–8; for Lucian and Ovid cf. Diggle loc. cit. (n. 73).

79. Cf. R. Heinze, *De Horatio Bionis imitatore* (diss. Bonn 1889) 10–11.

80. When Eros washes in Philetas' spring (2.5.4) we may be reminded of Prop. 3.3.51–2, *talia Calliope, lymphisque a fonte petitis| ora Philitea nostra rigauit aqua;* in view, however, of the traditional association of water with poetic inspiration (cf. A. Kambylis, *Die Dichterweihe und ihre Symbolik*, Heidelberg 1965), this need not be significant.

81. Note esp. 2.3.2 ἥκω δὲ ὑμῖν ὅσα εἶδον μηνύσων, ὅσα ἤκουσα ἀπαγγελῶν.

82. Cf. A. L. Wheeler, 'Propertius as Praeceptor Amoris' *CP* 5 (1910) 28–40, Murgatroyd's edition of Tibullus I, p. 130. Two examples of this character in the novel are Cleinias in Achilles Tatius (1.9–10) and the eunuch in Chariton (cf. above p. 34).

83. With Tib. 1.8.1–2 *non ego celari possum, quid nutus amantis| quidue ferant miti lenia uerba sono,* cf. D&C 3.15.4, πρότερον μὲν οὖν ἐκ νευμάτων καὶ γέλωτος συνεβάλετο.

84. Gow on Theocr. 3.2 discusses τίτυρος and notes the possibility that the Τίτυρος of that poem is in fact a goat; cf. n. 12 to Chap. 4.

85. T. G. Rosenmeyer, *The green cabinet* (Berkeley–Los Angeles 1969) 40-1 repeats the objection of A. Nowacki, *Philitae Coi fragmenta poetica* (diss. Münster 1927) 21 that if the Longan Philetas was intended to recall the Hellenistic poet, then his beloved ought to have been called Bittis, not Amaryllis; such a view ignores Longus' customary techniques of borrowing and imitation. There is, of course, no guarantee that Philitas did not in fact also write poetry about an Amaryllis. The Tityrus who is in love with an Amaryllis in *Eclogue* 1 is, like the Longan Philetas, a *senex* (vv. 46, 51).

86. For the spelling of the poet's name cf. J. Powell, *Collectanea Alexandrina* (Oxford 1925) p. 90; W. Crönert, 'Philitas von Kos' *Hermes* 37 (1902) 212-27; W. Kuchenmüller, *Philetae Coi reliquiae* (diss. Berlin 1928) 15-17. In our manuscripts the poet often appears as Φιλητᾶς and so the form of the name is no hindrance to an identification with the Longan character, an identification which goes back at least to R. Reitzenstein, *Epigramm und Skolion* (Giessen 1893) 260 n. 1.

87. For a play on the name Philetas cf. *AP* 11.218.3 (= *HE* 1373) where Dobree's Φιλητᾶ for the meaningless φίλιτρα is very attractive, cf. Kuchenmüller op. cit. 17. Pace Philippides [1978] 248-51, I see no reason to connect Φιλητᾶς with φιλήτης.

88. Cf. van Blumenthal, *RE* 19.2168-9; Gow's *Theocritus* II p. 130 n. 7.

89. Cairns [1979] 26.

90. Most recent editors accept *Coe* [Beroaldus] for the transmitted *dure*. Whatever the true reading, a reference to Philitas seems very likely.

91. Prop. 2.1.6, *hoc totum e Coa ueste uolumen erit*, is almost certainly a reference to Philitas; observe that Callimachus' *Aetia* is recalled in v. 3 of that poem, *non haec mihi cantat Apollo*.

92. Cf. Kuchenmüller op. cit. 28-37; A. W. Bulloch, *PCPS* n.s. 19 (1973) 84; M. Puelma, *MH* 39 (1982) 224-5. G. Scheibner, 'Ein unbekanntes Philitasfragment in der Berliner Papyrussammlung' in F. Zucker (ed.), *Menanders Dyskolos als Zeugnis seiner Epoche* (Berlin 1965) 103-14, publishes two broken columns from a narrative (with bucolic elements) in hexameters preserved on a papyrus of the late second or first century B.C. He ascribes the verses to Philitas on grounds of general suitability and a coincidence with fr. 6 Powell (= 2 Kuchenmüller), but this must be quite uncertain, although no better candidate for authorship has been forthcoming.

93. That Theocr. 11.1-3 is an echo of Philitas has also been suggested by Cairns [1979] 26 n. 116. For the φάρμακον topos in the novel cf. Chariton 6.3.7 (cf. above p. 34) and Stephanie West, *ZPE* 7

(1971) 95.

94. In mocking the notion that poetry can cure the νόσος of love Horace (*Sat.* 1.2.105–10) quotes another epigram of Callimachus (31 Pf. = *HE* 1035).

95. Cf. F. Cairns, 'Propertius 1.18 and Callimachus, *Acontius and Cydippe*' *CR* n.s. 19 (1969) 131–4 and P. Fedeli's commentary on 1.18 *passim.*

96. Cf. I. M. LeM. DuQuesnay, 'Vergil's First *Eclogue*' *Papers of the Liverpool Latin Seminar* 3 (1981) 29–182, pp. 38–51.

97. With 2.4.3, τοῦτο ποικίλον τι χρῆμα ἦν καὶ ἀθήρατον, O. Schönberger, *RhM* 119 (1976) 95–6, compares Clem. Alex. *Strom.* 2.2.5 and suggests that both authors echo a verse of earlier poetry. With 2.5.5, χαῖρε, μόνος ἀνθρώπων ἐν γήραι θεασάμενος τοῦτο τὸ παιδίον, Cairns [1979] 26 compares Call. fr. 1.37–8 Pf., but more relevant are Pl. *Symp.* 195a–b and the anecdote about Sophocles told at Pl. *R.* 1.329b–c, which was taken up by the rhetorical tradition as a good example of χρεία (cf. Theon II.66 Sp.).

98. 'From Polyphemus to Corydon' in West–Woodman (n. 64 above) 35–69, p. 60.

99. Cf. also Flower Smith on Tib. 2.5.30. Cairns [1979] 27 also notes this correspondence between Longus and Virgil and observes that it 'suggests that Philetas introduced this topos into Hellenistic poetry'.

100. Cf. also 3.23.4 μιμεῖται [sc. ἡ Γῆ] καὶ αὐτὸν συρίττοντα τὸν Πᾶνα. On μίμησις in *D&C* cf. above pp. 19–20.

101. The similarity is noted by Erika Simon, *MDAI(R)* 69 (1962) 153–4 and Cresci [1981] 22–3.

102. With 1.29.1 cf. also Theocr. 22.98–9, ἔστη δὲ πληγαῖς μεθύων, ἐκ δ' ἔπτυσεν αἷμα| φοίνιον. In an epigram of Leonidas (*AP* 7.657 = *HE* 2062) a dead shepherd asks his former companions to put flowers on his grave. This poem may have been in the back of Longus' mind, particularly as it is followed in the Anthology by a group of Theocritean epigrams (but cf. *HE* II p. 328 on the transmission).

103. Cf. F. Cairns, *Generic composition in Greek and Roman poetry* (Edinburgh 1972) 90–1; R. Nisbet and M. Hubbard's commentary on Horace, *Odes* II, p. 336.

104. 'Le dieu Amour chez Properce et chez Longus' *Bulletin de la classe des lettres et des sciences morales et politiques de l'Académie Royale de Belgique*⁵ 39 (1953) 263–70.

105. Cf. R. Nisbet and M. Hubbard's edition of Horace, *Odes* I, pp. 262–3.

106. There is a great deal of unsorted material in A. Spies, *Militat omnis amans: ein Beitrag zur Bildersprache der antiken Erotik*

(diss. Tübingen 1930). Of relevance to Longus are Plaut. *Merc.*
859–63, Ovid, *Am.* 2.16.19–30, *AA* 2.31–8, Tib. 1.2.27–30,
V. *Ecl.* 10.64–9 and Max. Tyr. 20.2b–c H which lists πῦρ,
θάλαττα, ποταμοὶ πάντες and χειμῶνες among the things which
yield to love; note also Philostr. *Epist.* 23 Benner–Fobes πλεῖν
κέλευσον, ἐμβαίνω· πληγὰς ὑπομεῖναι, καρτερῶ· ῥῖψαι τὴν
ψυχήν, οὐκ ὀκνῶ· δραμεῖν διὰ πυρός, οὐκ ἀναίνομαι.
107. Cf., e.g., Hor. *C.* 1.16.9–12, *Sat.* 1.1.39, 2.3.54–5, *Epist.* 1.1.46.
108. Cf., e.g., V. *Georg.* 3.349ff., Hor. *C.* 4.5.25; a glance at the
Concordance will show how often Ovid complains of the snows
and cold of Scythia.
109. For the evidence cf. A. Otto, *Die Sprichwörter und sprich-*
wörtlichen Redensarten der Römer (Leipzig 1890) *s.v.* Scytha.

Chapter Four

1. I have in general modelled my division of *clausulae* on S. Heibges,
De clausulis Charitoneis (diss. Halle 1911); my percentages refer
only to *clausulae* at sentence-end (i.e. at a major pause), but I
suspect that an examination of colon-ends would produce similar
results. With regard to vowels before mute plus liquid I followed
the flexible practice advocated by Heibges 57–9. The discussion
of prose rhythm in *D&C* by Philippides [1978] 153–67 seems to
me entirely wrong-headed.
2. Cf. Cic. *Orat.* 212, Norden [1898] I 135.
3. Valley [1926].
4. 'Pure' diction is defined as κοινὴ καὶ εἰς ἅπαντας ἤκουσα καὶ
μὴ τετραμμένη μηδ' ἀφ' ἑαυτῆς οὖσα σκληρά (Hermogenes p.
229.8 R).
5. The most relevant sections of Hermogenes περὶ ἀφελείας are
translated by D. A. Russell in D. A. Russell and M. Winterbottom,
Ancient literary criticism (Oxford 1972) 572–5.
6. Cf. Valley [1926] 101. προσκώπους in 2.12.1 may come from
Thucyd. 1.10.4 as it is not otherwise attested in the classical
period and Pollux 1.95 cites it from the historian; the word is,
however, used twice by Lucian (*Kataplous* 19, *Charon* 1). ὅπλα
κινεῖν in 3.1.1 probably echoes Thucyd. 1.82.1: I have not
found another example before Herodian 7.4.1, and the surrounding context in the novel would make such an echo appropriate.
At 3.2.3 ἀδεῶς ἐπιμίγνυσθαι καὶ κατὰ γῆν καὶ θάλασσαν is a clear
echo of Thucyd. 1.2.2 οὐδ' ἐπιμειγνύντες ἀδεῶς ἀλλήλοις οὔτε
κατὰ γῆν οὔτε διὰ θαλάσσης and at 3.1.2 καταλέξαντες ἀσπίδα
τρισχιλίαν καὶ ἵππον πεντακοσίαν κτλ. reflects the language of
military historians, cf. LSJ *s.v.* ἀσπίς I 2, *s.v.* ἵππος II.

7. My analysis inevitably owes a great deal to Luigi Castiglioni, 'Stile e testo del romanzo pastorale di Longo' *RIL* 61 (1928) 203-23. The use of tricola in Greek prose is also studied by Ed. Norden, *De Minucii Felicis aetate et genere dicendi* (Greifswald 1897) 35-47, especially p. 46 on Longus. Norden notes the popularity of this device with the sophists of the second century A.D.

8. Cf. 2.37.1 ὁ Δάφνις Πᾶνα ἐμιμεῖτο, τὴν Σύριγγα Χλόη.

9. For the text cf. M. L. West, *CQ* n.s. 12 (1962) 178-9. In Homer ἀγέλη is always used of cattle except at *Il*. 19.281 (horses).

10. διάχρυσος ('interwoven with gold') is used most naturally of material; ἐπίχρυσος is the standard term for 'gilded' (cf. A. Körte, *Hermes* 64 (1929) 267-70). Note that at Plut. *Mor*. 142c ὑποδήματα are διάχρυσα.

11. At 2.37.2 ποιήματα means both 'poems' and 'works'.

12. At Theocr. 3.2-4 ἐλαύνειν and ἄγειν both occur within three verses (cf. Gow on v. 2); if the implications of ὁ τίτυρος are ambiguous (cf. Gow loc. cit.), we might consider the possibility that there is a play on the sexual meaning of ἐλαύνειν (LSJ *s.v.* I 5).

13. For the collocation of σῦριγξ and σάλπιγξ cf. Pl. *R.* 3.397a, Max. Tyr. 26.4f H and note Ach. Tat. 3.2.2-3, ἀνέμων ποικίλων ἐσύριζε ψόφος· καὶ ὁ μὲν ἀὴρ εἶχε σάλπιγγος ἦχον.

14. For the use of νεανικός cf. Ar. *Wasps* 1307 and 1362 of the rejuvenated Philocleon. Reeve considers 3.6.1 corrupt because Daphnis was not really interested in the birds and he proposes either περιμένων for μεριμνῶν or ὄρνιθας ⟨περιμένων⟩ καὶ τὴν Χλόην μεριμνῶν. This seems to me an over-pedantic objection and the wit is quite Longan, cf. 4.6.2 μειράκιον ... εἰωθὸς αἶγας βλέπειν καὶ ὄρος [ὄις Hinlopen] καὶ γεωργοὺς καὶ Χλόην κτλ.

15. The pun was noted by Schäfer (cf. Seiler ad loc.). τραγικός 'goaty' is a rare and late word (Plutarch, Lucian), but for etymological fun with this word cf. already Pl. *Cratylus* 408c-d, Hor. *AP* 220 *carmine qui tragico uilem certauit ob hircum* etc.

16. The pun was first elucidated by C. Bonner, *CP* 2 (1907) 338-40; the text is also discussed by Valley [1926] 9; J. Edmonds, *CQ* 5 (1911) 94; J. Milliner, *REG* 88 (1975) xi and M. Brioso Sánchez, *Emerita* 45 (1977) 379-85 who believes that no pun is necessary to explain the text. The links between goats and the sea are explored by U. Pestalozza, *Nuovi saggi di religione mediterranea* (Florence 1964) 167-74.

17. I cannot share Reeve's doubts about the presence of this piece of verbal wit, although I would agree that the MSS' ᾄδοντα may be kept. Courier well compared Hor. *Sat.* 1.4.62 *disiecti membra*

poetae where, *pace* Kiessling–Heinze, a play on the two senses of *membrum* seems certain.

18. Cf. Σ Ar. *Knights* 782, Gomme–Andrewes–Dover on Thucyd. 7.41.2. I am not convinced by Lindsay (p. 103 n. 2 of his translation, cf. also D. N. Levin, *RSC* 25 (1977) 8 n. 11) that χήν at 3.16.3 means 'pudenda' as well as 'goose'.

19. Cf. Dover's edition of Theocritus pp. xlv–xlviii.

20. Cf. Norden [1898] I 134ff.

21. Cf. E. Rohde, 'Die asianische Rhetorik und die zweite Sophistik' *RhM* 41 (1886) 170-90 (= *Kleine Schriften* II 75-97); Norden [1898] I 407ff.; Bompaire [1958] 102-3.

22. Cf. Arist. *Rhet.* 3.1408b21-35, Dion. Hal. *de comp.* 25, Quint. 9.4.72-8; Cicero describes the short phrases of Gorgias and Thrasymachus as *uersiculorum similia* (*Orator* 39). Cf. in general Norden [1898] I 53-5.

23. Cf. Arist. *Rhet.* 3.1404a24-8, Norden [1898] I 52-3. Arist. *Rhet.* 3.1406a12-13 observes that one can, like Homer, say 'white milk' in poetry but not in prose. It is interesting that the scholiast on Theocr. 5.53 feels compelled to explain that when Theocritus writes λευκοῖο γάλακτος he does not imply that there is black milk, but simply that all milk is white φύσει.

24. Cf. Alcaeus 130.32-5 LP (= 130b.17-20 V); D. L. Page, *Sappho and Alcaeus* (Oxford 1955) 168 n. 4; Erbse on Σ Hom. *Il.* 9.129.

25. The text of Demosthenes has 'punish for murder'.

26. ἦ ῥα, καὶ ἀγκὰς ἔμαρπτε Κρόνου παῖς ἣν παράκοιτιν·
    τοῖσι δ' ὑπὸ χθὼν δῖα φύεν νεοθηλέα ποίην,
    λωτόν θ' ἑρσήεντα ἰδὲ κρόκον ἠδ' ὑάκινθον
    πυκνὸν καὶ μαλακόν, ὃς ἀπὸ χθονὸς ὑψόσ' ἔεργε.
    τῶι ἔνι λεξάσθην, ἐπὶ δὲ νεφέλην ἕσσαντο
    καλὴν χρυσείην· στιλπναὶ δ' ἀπέπιπτον ἔερσαι.

27. Editors of Herodotus generally accept Eldick's conjecture θολερῶι ('muddy') for the transmitted δολερῶι.

28. The origin of the hexameters is disputed, cf. Dover ad loc.: 'Perhaps the verses are meant to be understood as Agathon's own; but he may be quoting from a source not known to us.' Unfortunately Plato's use of ἐπέρχεται does not settle the matter: contrast *Phaedo* 88d with *Cratylus* 428c and *Gorgias* 485e.

29. Cf. Bompaire [1958] 444-6.

30. Cf. Max. Tyr. 4.4d, 18.4e H, Theon II.66.19 Sp., Men. Rhet. 334 Sp.-RW.

31. The first two books of Herodotus were a favourite source of διηγήματα μυθικά in the schools, cf. Theon II.67.4 Sp., K. -A. Riemann, *Das herodoteische Geschichtswerk in der Antike* (diss. Munich 1967) 112-13.

32. For the γλυκύτης of Herodotus cf. Dio Chrys. 18.10 Ἡροδότωι

μὲν οὖν, εἴ ποτε εὐφροσύνης σοι δεῖ, μετὰ πολλῆς ἡσυχίας ἐντεύξῃι· τὸ γὰρ ἀνειμένον καὶ τὸ γλυκὺ τῆς ἀπαγγελίας ὑπόνοιαν παρέξει μυθῶδες μᾶλλον ἢ ἱστορικὸν τὸ σύγγραμμα εἶναι, Men. Rhet. 389.27 Sp.–RW μεστὴ δὲ καὶ ἡ ἱστορία Ἡροδότου γλυκέων διηγημάτων, Quint. 10.1.73.

33. In his commentary on this passage of Hermogenes, Syrianus cites among examples of κάλλος χωρίου the garden of Alcinous in *Odyssey* 7 (p. 77.3 R) and Longus too exploits this famous passage cf. above p. 72.

34. Cf. Dion. Hal. *de comp.* 23; D. Hagedorn, *Zur Ideenlehre des Hermogenes* (Göttingen 1964) 52–3.

35. Cf. n. 43 to Chap. 2.

36. There is a useful discussion of the ancient theory of citation from poetry in Bompaire [1958] 382–404.

37. Cf. ὥσπερ εἰκὸς ἦν in 1.2.3 and parenthetic τὸ καινότατον in 3.30.2 and 4.22.3.

BIBLIOGRAPHY

G. Anderson, *Eros Sophistes: ancient novelists at play* (American Classical Studies 9, Chico, Ca. 1982)

J. Bompaire, *Lucien écrivain* (Paris 1958)

C. Bonner, 'On certain supposed literary relationships' *CP* 4 (1909) 32–44, 276–90

P. Borgeaud, *Recherches sur le dieu Pan* (Geneva 1979)

F. Cairns, *Tibullus: a Hellenistic poet at Rome* (Cambridge 1979)

G. Carugno, 'Alcifrone nei suoi rapporti con Longo e il mondo bucolico' *GIF* 8 (1955) 153–9

H. H. O. Chalk, 'Eros and the Lesbian Pastorals of Longus' *JHS* 80 (1960) 32–51

F. C. Christie, *Longus and the development of the pastoral tradition* (diss. Harvard 1972)

E. Courtney, 'Parody and literary allusion in Menippean satire' *Philologus* 106 (1962) 86–100

L. R. Cresci, 'Il romanzo di Longo Sofista e la tradizione bucolica' *Atene e Roma* n.s. 26 (1981) 1–25

G. Dalmeyda, 'Longus et Alciphron', *Mélanges Gustave Glotz* (Paris 1932) I 277–87

B. Effe, 'Longos. Zur Funktionsgeschichte der Bukolik in der römischen Kaiserzeit' *Hermes* 110 (1982) 65–84

Erotica Antiqua = B. P. Reardon (ed.), *Erotica Antiqua: Acta of the International Conference on the Ancient Novel* (Bangor 1977)

F. Garin, 'Su i romanzi Greci' *SIFC* 17 (1909) 423–60

A. Geyer, 'Roman und Mysterienritual' *WJA* n.f. 3 (1977) 179–96

E. Harlan, *The description of paintings as a literary device and its application in Achilles Tatius* (diss. Columbia 1965)

A. Heiserman, *The novel before the novel* (Chicago–London 1977)

W. Kroll, *Studien zum Verständnis der römischen Literatur* (Stuttgart 1924, 1964)

W. McCulloh, *Longus* (New York 1970)

R. Merkelbach, *Roman und Mysterium in der Antike* (Munich 1962)

M. Mittelstadt, *Longus and the Greek love romance* (diss. Stanford 1964)

    'Longus: *Daphnis and Chloe* and Roman narrative painting' *Latomus* 26 (1967) 752–61

    'Bucolic-lyric motifs and dramatic narrative in Longus' *Daphnis and Chloe*' *RhM* 113 (1970) 211–27

E. Norden, *Die antike Kunstprosa* (Leipzig 1898)

B. E. Perry, *The ancient romances* (Berkeley–Los Angeles 1967)

M. Philippides, *Longus: antiquity's innovative novelist* (diss. State University of New York 1978)

B. P. Reardon, *Courants littéraires grecs des IIe et IIIe siècles après J. -C.* (Paris 1971)

H. Reich, *De Alciphronis Longique aetate* (diss. Königsberg 1894)

E. Rohde, *Der griechische Roman und seine Vorläufer*[3] (Leipzig 1914)

G. Rohde, 'Longus und die Bukolik' *RhM* 86 (1937) 23–49 (= *Studien und Interpretationen*, Berlin 1963, 91–116)

A. M. Scarcella, 'Realtà e letteratura nel paesaggio sociale ed economico del romanzo di Longo Sofista' *Maia* 22 (1970) 103–31
'La tecnica dell' imitazione in Longo Sofista' *GIF* n.s. 2 (1971) 34–59

O. Schissel, 'Die Technik des Bildeinsatzes' *Philologus* 72 (1913) 83–114

E. L. Shields, *The cults of Lesbos* (diss. Johns Hopkins 1917)

G. Valley, *Über den Sprachgebrauch des Longus* (diss. Uppsala 1926)

P. G. Walsh, *The Roman novel* (Cambridge 1970)

G. Wojaczek, *Daphnis* (Meisenheim am Glan 1969)

INDEX OF PASSAGES DISCUSSED

INDEX OF SUBJECTS

135

Lesbos, 2–3, 21, 46, 91
Lollianus, Φοινικικά,1
Longus: date, 3–15; links with Lesbos,
   2–3, 21; prose rhythms in,
   3, 84–5; structure of *D&C*,
   5, 65–6; style, 3, 84–91;
   title of novel, 1–2; vocabulary
   of, 85
Lucian: imitated by Alciphron, 13
   n. 54; use of Latin authors,
   77
Lycaenion, character in *D&C*, 28,
   60–1, 68–9

Magnus of Nisibis, 51
medicine, 'sophistic', 51
Megacles, character in *D&C*, 6, 67
Menander, comic poet: *Dyscolus*,
   37, 69; *Periceiromene*, 67
metamorphosis, 54, 56 n. 121
mimesis, 19–20, 45–6, 73
money values, in *D&C*, 4
μῦθος, ancient concept of, 47
Myrtale, character in *D&C*, 17

Nape, character in *D&C*, 6, 17
novel, *D&C* as example of genre,
   63–6

Orpheus: and Eurydice, 76; Daphnis
   represented as, 9, 30–1; in
   art, 31; on Lesbos, 53–4

painting: and poetry, 44–7; links
   with *D&C*, 4–6; literary
   description of, 5, 38–9
Pan: and Dionysus, 37; and Pitys, 53;
   cosmic role of, 37; Daphnis
   likened to, 16; lover of
   Daphnis, 26
Petronius: parody in, 65; title of
   novel, 1
Philetas, character in *D&C*, 31–6,
   77–9
Philitas, Hellenistic poet: echoed
   by Longus, 76–83; form

of name, 78 n. 86; survival,
   78–9
Philoxenus, *Cyclops*, 79
pine-trees, in bucolic literature,
   9, 12–13
Plato: echoed by Longus, 32 n. 43,
   56–7; later influence of
   Phaedrus, 32 n. 43, 97; later
   influence of *Symposium*,
   32 n. 47, 91, 96; view of
   poetry, 45, 50
Plautus, *Casina*, 70–1
pleasure, as object of poetry, 47–50
Pratinas, 10
prologue, of *D&C*, 38–52

Sappho: echoed by Longus, 62,
   73–6; leap from cliff, 29;
   style, 97
Scythia, proverbially harsh climate
   of, 83
Simias, Πτέρυγες, 36 n. 56
slaves, cost of, 4
Stoics, 18, 46 n. 90
Syrinx, myth of, 52–7

Theocritus: echoed by Longus, 25–6,
   29, 56, 59–63, 71, 74, 76,
   78–82; natural world in,
   21; studied in second century
   A.D., 4
Thucydides: echoed by Longus, 4
   n. 18, 85 n. 6; later influence
   of, 48–9
Tibullus, similarities with Longus,
   5–6, 21
Tityrus, character in *D&C*, 78
Triphiodorus, date of, 76

Virgil, possibly echoed by Greek
   writers, 76–7, 81–2

Xenophon of Ephesus, title of
   novel, 1–2

Zeno of Cyprus, 51

For EU product safety concerns, contact us at Calle de José Abascal, 56–1°, 28003 Madrid, Spain or eugpsr@cambridge.org.

www.ingramcontent.com/pod-product-compliance
Ingram Content Group UK Ltd.
Pitfield, Milton Keynes, MK11 3LW, UK
UKHW012339130625
459647UK00009B/391